Reaction to 1829 *St. Matthew Passion* Performance[1]

"*I must tell you about what in this moment fills my whole soul, and that is the Passion music of Sebastian Bach. I count the hearing of it to be among those pleasures of which you once spoke in reference to Lear: that it should be granted to humanity to experience such a work of art, that is something great and ennobling!*"

JOHANN WILHELM LOEBELL TO JOHANN TIECK

"*I have been thinking about your report on the successful performance of that great old piece of music and for me it is as though I could hear in the distance the ocean singing.*"

JOHANN WOLFGANG VON GOETHE TO CARL FRIEDRICH ZELTER

[the chorus] "*. . . was possessed by a fire, a pulsating force and at the same time a heartrending tenderness, which I have never before heard in them. The overflowing hall gave the impression of a church: the deepest quiet and the most solemn reverence seized the gathering; one heard only a few involuntary exclamations of deeply stirred feeling; what is said so often without justification may truly be said of this undertaking, that an extraordinary spirit, a universal, transcendent interest, guided it.*"

FANNY MENDELSSOHN (MEMBER OF THE CHORUS)

THE SACRED SACRIFICE

*Cultivating Lenten Traditions
with Bach's Great Passion*

Hannah Paris

BLUE SKY
DAISIES

The Sacred Sacrifice: Cultivating Lenten Traditions with Bach's Great Passion
Copyright © 2024 Hannah Paris
Published by Blue Sky Daisies
       Wichita, Kansas
Cover Design by Blue Sky Daisies © 2024
BlueSkyDaisies.net

The *St. Matthew Passion* German libretto reproduced in this volume, by Johann Sebastian Bach and Christian Friderich Henrici, nom de plume Picander, c. 1725, is in the public domain. The English translation of *St. Matthew Passion* included in this volume is by Hannah Paris copyright © 2024.

Image credit: Johann Sebastian Bach, Matthäuspassion BWV 244, Autograph von Nr. 71. Public domain. Digital faithful reproduction from wikipedia commons: https://commons.wikimedia. org/wiki/File:BWV_244_Nr._71.svg

Cover Image (cross and greenery): SvetaArtStore via Creative Market

Poetry selections reproduced in this book are in the public domain.

Unless otherwise indicated, all Scripture quotations are taken from The Holy Bible, King James Version (KJV).

Scripture quotations taken from the (NASB®) New American Standard Bible®, Copyright © 1960, 1971, 1977, 1995 by The Lockman Foundation. Used by permission. All rights reserved. lockman.org

Scripture quotations marked (ESV) are from The ESV® Bible (The Holy Bible, English Standard Version®), copyright © 2001 by Crossway, a publishing ministry of Good News Publishers. Used by permission. All rights reserved.

All links were active at the time of publication, but are subject to change over time.

Paperback ISBN-13: 978-1-944435-39-4
Hardcover ISBN-13: 978-1-944435-40-0

THE SACRED
SACRIFICE

Contents

Introduction

A signature floral Laura Ashley dress scratched my neck where it cinched tight, and I glanced sideways at my sister in her matching attire to see if she was feeling it too. The sheer black stockings covering my legs felt uncomfortably tight on my tummy, and my shoes were stiff. I sighed as sweat gathered behind my neck under my labored-over hair, undoubtedly frizzing it out. Why had I even tried with all those heating elements? This hair would not be tamed. My eyes wandered around the auditorium as I tried to distract myself from the physical discomforts by taking in what faces I could in the dim light. Music as familiar to me as the latest Disney soundtrack filled every inch of space. My sister scrunched up next to me on the pew, and I could already feel her body relaxing against mine settling into the annual *Messiah* slump. She would be asleep soon. I would follow her shortly with the image of my parents' joyful faces stamped on my mind.

Handel's *Messiah* was a constant in our house from the time Christmas music started until New Year's Day when the decorations came down. It played in our Volvo when Mom picked me up from school, the car smelling of leather and cinnamon Dentyne gum. If Sandi Patty and Wayne Watson were coming to Charlotte, North Carolina with the Young Messiah production, we'd be there. Every year my parents would find a live performance and every year, no matter how hard we tried, both my sister and I fell asleep, her head on my shoulder and my head on the cold wood at the end of the pew. When the "Hallelujah" chorus began and the audience rose to their feet as one body, we would find ourselves jarred into alertness. After clearing our heads from the blood rush, we finished our annual tradition by giggling quietly together at yet another year of being brutally awakened by one of the most phenomenal musical compositions in history. Eventually, we joined everyone in singing, but really, we simply didn't have the ears to hear its crushing beauty at the time.

I wanted that for my own children. I wanted Handel's *Messiah* to be deeply familiar to them and part of the rhythm of Christmas. I also wanted my girls to love the words and understand the structure. I wanted to give them the ears to hear, if I possibly could. When I married, my husband and I almost immediately began merging our Christmas traditions to create a season of expectation for ourselves and our children. Naturally, that meant incorporating the timeless oratorio. For the first few years, I took my mom's route and played it often and everywhere. Then I heard tale of Cindy Rollins's *Hallelujah: Cultivating Advent Traditions with Handel's Messiah*. It sounded like exactly what I needed to help all of us dig deep into both the music itself, and Advent as a whole; to quietly and with the beauty of art draw us into Christmas morning prepared to worship. Our years of following Rollins's listening guide have been full and peaceful. The girls know the *Messiah* better and better each year, remembering background details and looking forward to lesser-known songs that they know and love because it sounds like sheep frolicking or roads going crooked. Two years of hyper-prepped hearts for Christmas through Advent were followed by Easters that snuck up and caught us totally unprepared.

My Story

It would probably be worthwhile for me to back up a bit and explain our lives. I have lived my entire adult life either preparing to be in Papua New Guinea, in Papua New Guinea, or taking a break from Papua New Guinea (PNG). PNG is on an island that sits just north of Australia. The island itself is called New Guinea, but PNG only takes up half while the other side is part of Indonesia. Quite recently we moved down to Australia, but for many years we lived in a tiny township on the northern coast, just shy of the equator. Every day felt like every other day with very little to communicate a change in season or nearness of holidays. Although this is slowly beginning to change, the stores don't announce what holiday is next with decorations and merchandise. The churches don't plan far ahead and certainly don't have Passion plays and events planned weeks in advance. As well-prepared for Christmas Day as we always tried to be, Easter was the complete opposite. A couple of years ago when the church bell started clanging non-stop across the street from our house at sunrise announcing another Easter I was unaware had already arrived, I had had it. How could I be so intentional about Christmas and so lackadaisical about Easter when Easter is the more important of the two? Instead, here I was finding myself scrambling year after year to get the kids "in the mood" and full of "somber understanding" and "He is Risen rejoicing" and whatever else I guiltily felt was lacking. Needless to say, the girls bemusedly played along, but clearly were not getting a depth of understanding about Easter. My frustration led me directly to the age-old church calendar and the Lenten season, both long neglected in my own faith life.

Advent came naturally to me as I love all things Christmas, but it has only been in my own maturation of understanding that it's being teased apart from the general feel-goods of Christmas and put into its context inside the church liturgical calendar. The roots of Advent being a somber time of fasting and darkness before the twinkly lights and feasting of the twelve days is quite new to me. We don't adhere to it exactly like that, and there are so many iterations people follow now. However, it was an organic addition to our Christmas traditions that brought into clear focus the quiet of the season while we continued to allow for the twinkly lights earlier than the twelve days.

Lent had a bigger learning curve for me. It's longer, for one thing, and I'm starting from scratch. The framework of observance wasn't already there like it was at Christmastime. Lent is even more somber than Advent, a stoic preparation of our hearts for the celebration of Easter through lament and ashes. Feasting will happen, but not on this side of Christ's death. Here in the precursor to celebrating his victory over death, we are reminded of the darkness and waiting we endure. We are still on this side of our own deaths. We are still on this side of his second coming. We are still on this side of the New Earth. We are still on this side of Eternity. And here on this side it is dark and broken and lonely. While Advent gives us deep anticipation of the coming restoration, Lent reminds us of the "not yet" and impending death. Finally, Eastertide brings us into the light of his victory reminding us again of what will be.

> While Advent gives us deep anticipation of the coming restoration, Lent reminds us of the "not yet" and impending death.

As a Protestant, Lent was not practiced (and even a bit feared) in my church, but as soon as I started understanding what exactly it was and how to follow it, I felt I had found part of a solution.

Living in Papua New Guinea meant living near nature. It's hot. Brutally and unrelentingly hot. The humidity is constantly at the "you're swimming through air" level (a category I'm sure should be scientific), and so fans or wind are a necessity; otherwise, you're definitely swimming, but it's not in anything nice. The windows of our house stayed open to allow every breath of wind in, but with that sweet air came piles of dust. I found myself sweeping a lot. It's a grind and not my favorite, but silty floors are less my favorite. As technology became more widely available in PNG and the internet boomed, I started gaining access to podcasts. I was only around ten years late to the game, but when you live on the edge of Earth you end up being behind on a few things from back home. Sweeping became a time for me to step away from homeschooling and general parenting, and completely zone out. Headphones in and podcast on, I got some alone time with the broom.

The *St. Matthew Passion* Project

In 2021, I spent that alone time with Joy Clarkson's podcast *Speaking with Joy*. I heard an episode completely devoted to Bach's *St. Matthew Passion* just as I was educating myself on Lent and how I could organize some observance of it for our family. Joy played several stunning portions from the piece as she analyzed and pontificated brilliantly on its beauty. I was overwhelmed. This was it. This was the key. I scoured the internet hoping to find a listening guide through Lent using *St. Matthew Passion* to pair up with Cindy Rollins's guide through Advent using Handel's *Messiah*. Alas, there was none to be found.

I spent the next year researching and planning just how this could be done for our family. I'm a homeschooling mom of three littles (read: very busy), and we had several critical incidences on the field that disrupted our lives mentally, emotionally, and physically. Over the following year I pored through Bach's work, listening again and again, trying to sort out just how to do a German oratorio for small children. I swam in those musical waters and healed. Bach is able to bring us down to the darkest recesses of sorrow through the contrapuntal and gut-wrenching power of his music, which helped me begin to heal from my own raw wounds left untended after the wholly unexpected death of a friend. Everything about this project was life-giving for me.

I quickly surmised that breaking down Bach's work would be a tad more complicated than the *Messiah*. The most obvious difference is the source material. *St. Matthew Passion* is German, not English. There are plenty of English performances and translations, but each one has its own flare, and they have made their own translation choices. For another, it's a narrative that follows particular rules locked in from years of church history and the production of Passions for Good Friday services. Bach broke some rules and expectations with his *St. Matthew Passion*—much to the chagrin of his higher-ups—that I'll get into later on, but it still follows a very set pattern. I needed to figure out how to break up a storied composition into tiny listening morsels that was never meant to be broken up.

That initial listening guide broke down the Leonard Bernstein-led 1963 abridged English performance. My children had the English libretto in front of them to better understand the songs. We walked through it alongside about a dozen other families who agreed to try it out with us. When Easter morning arrived, we were rejoicing deeply and quietly after the emotional journey we just took, inching our way through the Last Supper, the Garden of Gethsemane, the arrest, crucifixion, and burial. Swinging back on Easter morning to listen to portions of Part 3 from Handel's *Messiah* brought our family full circle to Christmas, rooting us to our inextricable state of being as God's people living in the not yet. We are waiters, and we wait in anticipation of the renewal.

> Children are more than capable of appreciating the art, though it may take time and practice to get them there.

My goal was always to move into the German, unabridged and pure. Children are more than capable of appreciating the art, though it may take time and practice to get them there. The main listening guide in this book follows the unabridged German libretto and provides a parallel English translation.

Welcome to the world of Bach, a deeply religious and totally irascible man who did not let his talents go to waste.

Hannah Paris
Soli Deo Gloria

Cultivating Lenten Traditions with Bach's Great Passion

What is Lent?

Jesus fasted for forty days in the wilderness while preparing to begin his ministry. He took the time to feel physical discomfort, face extreme temptation, and lean on the strength of God to move from acting as man alone to announcing himself through ministry as fully God and fully man. The heart of Lent is to imitate Jesus's example and in prayer, penitence, and physical discomfort ready ourselves for Eastertide. It's an opportunity to suppress our wants and tendency to lean towards excess while feeding our spiritual lives as we wait to celebrate Jesus's redemptive act. Nowhere in the Bible does it mandate the observance of Lent. Instead, we choose to participate in the season to help prepare our hearts for celebrating Easter. At no point should it become an act alone nor should it become master.

Lent and Eastertide are traditions practiced by many different denominations and in varying ways. It can be confusing, especially if your church background really only highlights Easter/Resurrection Sunday. I'll try and break it down simply, but understand that this is simplistic and not accurate to all church denominations. Bach composed his work for use in the German Lutheran church with the *St. Matthew Passion* slotting into their Lenten traditions.

Since the *Passion* was conceived under this framework, we will follow the Lutheran liturgical calendar. Lent begins on Ash Wednesday with the collective remembrance of our temporal existence and need for repentance and ends on Holy Saturday just before Easter Sunday. Woven into Lent is Holy Week (also called Passion week) and the Paschal Triduum. Throughout the weeks of Lent, Sundays are breaks in the fast that give us periodic glimpses of the feasting to come during Eastertide. It's a constant reminder that we live in the not-yet-but-already-here of Christ's kingdom.

> Nowhere in the Bible does it mandate the observance of Lent. Instead, we choose to participate in the season to help prepare our hearts for celebrating Easter.

Holy Week is overlaid onto Lent as the last week leading up to Easter Sunday. It starts on Palm Sunday and includes Holy Monday through Wednesday followed by Maundy Thursday, Good Friday, and Holy (or Black) Saturday. Lent officially ends on Holy Saturday. The Paschal Triduum, or the three Easter days, straddles the last days of Lent and Easter Sunday. The Triduum begins Maundy Thursday evening and finishes at the evening service on Easter Sunday. More information on Ash Wednesday, the Holy Week days, and the Paschal Triduum, both how they are traditionally observed and how you can observe them in your home, are included in the following listening guide.

Fasting is foundational to the observance of Lent. Our family fasts together and, right now, to a very minimal degree. It has become more popular in recent decades to fast from anything, not necessarily food. Technically, "fasting" from things other than food is called abstinence. We understand why people choose to abstain from all manner of habits and technology, but we believe fasting from food and feeling the consequence of it as physical discomfort in our bellies is Scripturally important; as we hunger for food, so should we hunger for God and so should we trust God to satiate. Our children are unpracticed in fasting from food, so we started light and will increase our expectations each year. Our method could be a good way for your family to start, too, but as all things in this book are meant to do, our ideas about fasting are included here to inspire you and not to be legalistic. Create a plan that suits your family, then go to the Bible and your church leadership to ground that plan. No matter how you choose to fast or what you choose to fast (or abstain) from, it's important that you don't allow it to become a purely performative act. Our children need to understand the goals of fasting during Lent, which means their parents need to know those goals.

Again, this fasting plan is where we started knowing we would slowly intensify throughout the years. Each week we fast from two meals and spend that time praying through a liturgy from Douglas McKelvey's book *Every Moment Holy*. During Holy Week we elim-

Monday	Tuesday	Wednesday	Thursday	Friday	Saturday	Sunday
Week 1	Shrove Tuesday	1 Ash Wednesday: Lent Begins	2	3	4	Break Fast
5 Week 2	6	7	8	9	10	Break Fast
11 Week 3	12	13	14	15	16	Break Fast
17 Week 4	18	19	20	21	22	Break Fast
23 Week 5	24	25	26	27	28	Break Fast
29 Week 6	30	31	32	33	34	Palm Sunday (Holy Week Begins)
35 Holy Monday	36 Holy Tuesday	37 Holy Wednesday	38 Maundy Thursday	39 Good Friday	40 Holy (Black) Saturday	**Easter Sunday!** He is Risen!
				---------Triduum---------------		
------------------------Holy Week------------------------						

Devotional Plan Day Numbers Indicated; Forty Days of Fasting Excludes Sundays

inate most lights in the evening hours to live in physical darkness. We use booklights and candlelight to make our way through supper, showers, Holy Week activities, and bedtime routines, but we grope around quite a bit. We find that our entire family, Mom and Dad included, yearn for Easter Sunday when the lights return!

During Holy Week we eliminate most lights in the evening hours in order to live in physical darkness.

This brings us straight up to the oratorio itself. I'll take you on a brief walk through the immense history of *St. Matthew Passion* in the next section, and throughout the guide you'll find more detailed background information or devotional thoughts pertinent to that day's listening.

Why St. Matthew Passion?

I met Bach as a young musician learning both violin and piano. Bach and I had a complicated relationship, and some of his compositions left my music stand the worse for the wear. If I may be so bold as to admit, the second violin part for "Bach Double" ended up with a jagged hole right through the middle when I turned my violin bow into a spear in a fit of frustration. Unfortunately, I'm prone to an explosive nature. One thorn in my side is being a person of quite serious temperament with exacting expectations of myself and others, and a bad temper. It took growing up and losing some of my bitterness towards Bach for his difficult passages to find out he was a lot like me.

The myth of Bach as a poor cantor slaving away at masterpieces in a corner of Saxony for the glory of God alone is saint-like, but not totally true. He was a poor cantor, he did write masterpieces, and he was deeply religious, but he was also oh-so-very human. He was an ambitious, temper-prone, button-pushing, boundary testing swirl of creative energy and rage. He was demanding and a snipe. One quite famous anecdote about him was when he threw his wig at the organist in a fit of rage at the man's mistakes and told him, "You should have been a cobbler!"[2] He did fall into some manner of obscurity for a time, but his ambitions in life were very real and very motivating to him. When we strip away the false idea of Bach as a calm and quiet, saint-like individual drawing the music of angels from an organ, we put the humanity back into his masterpieces. We return to his works the power to move us mere mortals.

Johann Sebastian Bach

Bach was born into what scholars refer to as "The Class of 1685."[3] Within that one year, the world received three greats: Johann Sebastian Bach, George Frideric Handel, and Domenico Scarlatti. Each of these musical giants would play their parts in history determined by their families, skills, personalities, and sensibilities, but our focus here will be on Bach. Suffice it to say that Bach was born into an era of musical renown and into a family of musical royalty. He had layers of uncles and cousins and brothers in the professional world of music, from composing to performing to making instruments.[4] There was very little question when he was a child about what he would do later in life, but we don't know much about what type of boy he was.[5] The environment he was raised in after being orphaned at ten was known to be volatile. At first, he was with an exacting older brother, and then he moved into the world of church schools. The church schools and boys' choirs were rife with a culture of abuse, bullying, and hooliganism that went back years before Bach arrived on the scene. In fact, the street brawling between two warring choir schools got so bad in Lüneburg between the years 1655-1663 that the town council considered calling in soldiers to get the two gangs of singing teenagers under control.[6] I chuckled a bit when I first learned about it, but these were quite dangerous boys prone to doing some pretty violent things.

We don't know if Bach was a victim of this culture or part of the mayhem. Given his eruptive temperament it's distinctly possible that he spent his youth in these schools as part of the problem and repented of it later, but we just don't know.[7] Eventually, Bach's deeply religious sensibilities settled into his core being, and that most certainly grew out of a childhood surrounded by the teachings of the church. He eventually, though not always happily, chose a job centered on shepherding congregants through music, focusing his creative energy on sacred works rather than moving in the secular worlds and music that Handel embraced.[8]

Bach not only wrestled with his temper throughout life, but we know he also faced deep grief. His first meaningful brush with death was when he was six and his brother died. From then on, and in quick succession, he saw his large immediate family dwindle until he was orphaned at age ten. Later in life Bach's first wife

Why is it called *St. Matthew Passion*?

Many people mistakenly call this piece by Bach *St. Matthew's Passion*, but in fact, the proper short name is *St. Matthew Passion*. Or, it is sometimes shortened to "Bach's *Passion*" or "Bach's great *Passion*."

The full name of the oratorio was given by Bach in Latin, *"Passio Domini Nostri J[esus] C[hristus] Secundum Evangelistam Matthaeum,"* which means, **"The Passion of Our Lord Jesus Christ according to the Gospel of Matthew."** The Latin *passio*

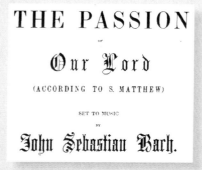

THE PASSION

OF

Our Lord

(ACCORDING TO S. MATTHEW)

SET TO MUSIC

BY

John Sebastian Bach.

means "to suffer." Indeed, it is Christ who suffered, and this moving piece tells of our Lord's passion following Matthew's narrative.

The word "passion" has been redefined in our culture in such a way that it's difficult to not think of passionate love. In a sense, that very much still works. It is God's passionate love for us that landed Christ in the midst of his passion—his suffering and death.

died while he was on a work trip. He left her whole and healthy, but he returned to her dead and buried. It's hard to imagine what that kind of trauma is like, having no warning whatsoever, on top of all the grief from childhood he was already carrying. Not only all of that, but he endured the deaths of numerous children, far more than was expected even during this time of high infant mortality. He was orphaned young and raised by his brother and the church schools full of hooligans. Grief and wrath seemed to be his constant companions.

We find Bach, a middle-aged man, living in a tiny apartment with his second wife and brood of children when he wrote *St. Matthew Passion*. He was working as Cantor, the modern equivalent of a worship leader, at the Thomaskirche (St. Thomas Church) in Leipzig where the rare common ground he found with his bosses, the Leipzig Council, was that he wasn't especially excited to work there, and they weren't especially excited to have him. His career in Leipzig was riddled with tense relations; the Leipzig Council is on record saying, "The Cantor was incorrigible."[9]

The ongoing conflict between Bach and the Council was rooted in his artistic expertise and desire to create impeccable music. He didn't want amateurs telling him what to do about his own work. On the other side was a long history of the Council having control over the cantors. Bach, with his well-established history of bucking authority, did not accept their state of affairs, and so went years of tense relations. John Eliot Gardiner states, "Aged twenty-one, Bach seems to have been a man of restive intelligence, heading for a life of more or less perpetual 'vexation and hindrance' (his own expression)—of a typical square peg in a round hole."[10]

When framed around his grief, the toxic work environment he was under, and his temper, the *St. Matthew Passion*, or what his family commonly referred to as his "great Passion,"[11] comes alive with a new depth of meaning.

Bach worked with Christian Friderich Henrici, whose pen name was Picander, on the libretto. Picander wrote the libretto

Part One

MATTHEW 26:1-56

Jesus Anointed

Judas's Bargain of Betrayal

The Last Supper

The Garden of Gethsemene

Jesus is Arrested

Part Two

MATTHEW 26:57-27:66

Jesus before the High Priest

Peter Denies Jesus

Judas's Remorse

Jesus before Pilate

Jesus Is Crucified

while Bach chose when and where to insert the chorales (German Lutheran hymns). It's a work of pain and sorrow, but even more so a declaration of repentance and hope that even as broken and pitiful as we, the human race, find ourselves to be, Jesus loved us enough.

The Structure of the Great Passion

In general, *St. Matthew Passion* is referred to as an oratorio, but in reality, that is not what it is; it's a work that defies boxes, and intentionally so.[12] In it, we see Bach playing with the limits of the rules set forth in his contract with the town council. He was forbidden from making anything too long and definitely, absolutely no operas. *St. Matthew Passion* can clock in at over three hours depending on the tempo chosen, and it far surpasses the drama that the Leipzig Council was trying to gatekeep with the "no operas" stipulation. Bach's Great Passion exceeds the scale of operas being written at the time by including chorales, and so cannot be classified as an opera. He sticks to the rules of the contract while simultaneously breaking them with his immense capacity to create.[13]

Two parts. The *Passion* is split into two parts that would have been separated by a sermon during the Good Friday service. The entirety of the work consists of a progression of actions and associated scenes. Each scene ends with a song (or songs) of reflection

BWV

BACH-WERKE-VERZEICHNIS

- Published in 1950
- Divided into 78 Movements
- Bernstein Recording

NBA

NEUE BACH-AUSGABE

- Published in 1954
- Divided in 68 Movements
- Gardiner Recording
- Klemperer Recording
- Suzuki Recording

that become part of the didactic teaching Bach and Picander are unabashedly trying to achieve in the work.

The response numbers guide the congregants in what to think and feel at various points in the narrative and can show up as recitatives, arias, or chorales.[14]

Recitatives are dialogue sung with rhythms and tempo that match normal talking speed while arias, though also used to propel the story forward in dialogue, move much slower.

Arias give the soloists opportunities to showcase their talent both through the complexity of what was written for them, and through the freedom they are given to improvise and make it their own.

You will also hear **chorales** intended to pull the audience into the story for a moment of collective sorrow and lament. Chorales are hymns usually associated with the German Lutheran Church. The chorale as seen in Bach's cantatas and passions were somewhat well-known hymns in the church at that time. The expectation was that the audience would join the choir singing the chorale, but there is some debate as to whether or not that happened in those early performances. By including the chorales, Bach is forcing the congregation into oneness with the story outside of time. It happened long ago, but it applies and impacts us today.

The Numbering Systems

You'll note throughout the listening guide that each track has two numbers associated with it. One numbering system, published in 1950 and called the Bach-Werke-Verzeichnis (BWV) or Bach Works Catalogue, divided the *Matthew Passion* into 78 numbers. Shortly thereafter in 1954, another catalogue was published called the Neue Bach-Ausgabe (NBA) or New Bach Edition. This catalogue divided the *Passion* into 68 numbers.[15] Since Bach and Picander did not divide the actions and scenes up originally, it can now be confusing when selecting a performance to use if you're accustomed to one numbering system over another. Some musical or artistic directors choose to follow the BWV and some the NBA. Therefore, I've included both numbering systems with each track so you can navigate any performance you choose to use.

Now that you have your footing on who Bach was and what kind of environment the *St. Matthew Passion* came out of, you should be ready to dive into the work with open ears. Almost all of the days in the guide have some amount of background information on what Bach and Picander were jointly doing in that portion of the oratorio.

How to Use This Guide

The plan laid out in this book is meant to be a guide through Lent, not a taskmaster. Use as much or as little of it as you would like. Glance over the background information and activities included in most days before sitting down with your family. Be aware that Saturdays and Sundays have read-alouds, poetry, music, or episodes from various shows, but no selections from the oratorio. Feel free to include those days or to take total breaks from the plan. The recommended readings, poetry, songs, and shows that surround the oratorio are additional ideas to enrich your coming weeks, but not integral to the plan itself.

You may start this guide and have high expectations for what your kids can absorb. Keep in mind, though, that it is an oratorio from the Baroque Era. If they aren't accustomed to this style of music, then asking them to sit and listen without complaint will be a tall order. It will be especially difficult for young children who can't follow along with the libretto. If your children clearly aren't on board with all this, don't despair! You can rework the schedule to suit your family and cut way back on the song selections. Even if your children are getting just a glimpse of this work, it's still a glimpse!

I also suggest helping your children become comfortable with this style of music, especially this particular work, before you move into Lent. Take a note out of my mom's playbook and turn on the oratorio in the background when you're cooking, driving, reading quietly, or any number of other times. They won't even realize that their ears are getting used to it, but when they sit down to listen, it will feel like a familiar friend rather than an inaccessible and complex bit of strange music that they "should" like.

Listening to *St. Matthew Passion*

Any of the following recorded performances can be found on streaming services. Another option is to use the Spotify playlist I created called "The Sacred Sacrifice." You will find the John Elliot Gardiner German performance, all the extra songs recommended on the weekends, and the Leonard Bernstein English performance in this playlist. (See page 202 for a link to this playlist.)

A word of warning: the playlist and any of these albums on a streaming service can be frustrating as the plan goes along because you can't see track numbers. Instead, you have to count down the tracks to find your spot or make an educated guess as to where you're landing that day. If this seems too annoying, you can buy any of these performances as a CD allowing you to manipulate the tracks quickly and easily.

The daily listening in this book refers to track numbers and running time from the Gardiner-Monteverdi Choir recording.

John Elliot Gardiner—German

John Elliot Gardiner's 1988 production alongside The English Baroque Soloists and The Montiverdi Choir is widely considered one of the best recordings out there. The daily listening in this book refers to the track numbers and running time from the Gardiner recording.

Gardiner, the soloists, and the ensemble had a clear vision and united direction for this unabridged interpretation of the *Matthew Passion*. It intentionally has a brisker tempo which, according to Lederer, brings form and shape to what can begin to feel cumbersome and lumpy if done too slowly.[16] Gardiner wanted to communicate the dramatic and emotional depth of the work by instilling a sense of urgency in the speed. This is the primary recording used in the implementation of this listening guide.

Otto Klemperer—German

Klemperer's production of the oratorio is rather the opposite approach to Gardiner. If you prefer something slower and more deliberate, this is the version for you. For comparison, the first number in Gardiner's performance is seven minutes long, while the same number in Klemperer's version is almost twelve minutes. That's not a difference in the source material. Gardiner chose a faster tempo throughout while Klemperer goes far slower.

Masaaki Suzuki—German

Suzuki conducts the Bach Collegium Japan in this production that doesn't sound nearly as big or dramatic as the other recordings. He used a smaller ensemble and orchestra for an interpretation of the piece that more closely resembles the original performances. It's a softer effect that may be a good choice for later years. I think when first engaging with the oratorio you should listen to a fuller, more dramatic performance since our ears are more accustomed to large sounds. However, after listening to what it would have sounded like during the Mendelssohn resurgence 100 years after its first performance when choices were intentionally made to enlarge the choirs and orchestras, it is thought provoking to hear a vastly different take from a completely different part of the world.[17] Bach is not just for Germany or Western Europe or the English-speaking nations. His impact is global and the Bach Collegium Japan, founded and led by Masaaki Suzuki, have demonstrated that again and again with stunning recordings of much of his work.

Leonard Bernstein—English

When I first became acquainted with *St. Matthew Passion* it immediately put me on my back foot. Oratorios are ever so close to operas, and operas are something I struggle to understand and enjoy.

I want to, but if I'm honest that's only because something inside tells me I should enjoy them. In the end they intimidate me, and this Passion in all its depth and majesty felt far out of my ability to appreciate. I couldn't understand any of the German words, and really, even when I listened in English I struggled to catch what they were saying. Bach does an absolutely phenomenal job of bringing the emotional heft of the story to bear with the music alone, and the familiar strains of "O Sacred Head, Now Wounded" left my heart aching. However, I thought if I (and my children) could only understand the words, they would resonate deep in our souls. I just knew it could draw us into the story and into Easter in the same way Handel's *Messiah* draws us toward Christmas Day throughout Advent. I was somewhat right. When I found the Leonard Bernstein-led English performance with the libretto and made my first listening plan for our family with it, we didn't look back. Now the piece in its original German speaks to us more clearly than the English, and we bask in the brief lifting of the veil that gives us a glimpse of the divine.

> [In the final track] Bernstein himself takes some time to analyze the oratorio and explain what's happening at certain points in the music... It's well worth a listen.

Bernstein recorded his abridged version of *St. Matthew Passion* in 1963. One thing I really appreciate about this version, beyond its remarkable execution, is the final track. Bernstein himself takes some time to analyze the oratorio and explain what's happening at certain points in the music. It's about fifteen minutes long and well worth a listen. This production is included at the end of "The Sacred Sacrifice" Spotify playlist created for this book (see page 202) in case you want your family to hear a worthy English production, but since it is abridged it will not follow this guide.

The Libretto

Picander wrote this masterpiece in his mother tongue, German. The text of *St. Matthew Passion*, like the text of all operas, is termed the *libretto*, a word that means "book." Most performances are sung in the original German. The original German libretto with my own simplified English translation is included in each day's entry.

There are many English translations readily available online that are fuller than what you will find here, but they are much too formal for small ears. The goal of this book is to help children absorb the words in a meaningful way, and that cannot happen if the language is too high. With that in mind, I intentionally created a translation your children can grasp. Please eventually go and get a richer English translation once you feel sufficiently familiar with the oratorio.

Companion Books

As you go through this Lenten devotional, readings from the following books are suggested. For the complete experience, please have these books on hand.

Leonard, Tom. *Becoming Bach*. Roaring Book Press, 2017.
A beautiful picture book biography about Bach's life.

Lewis, C. S. *The Lion, the Witch, and the Wardrobe*. Geoffrey Bless, 1950.
The first (in publication order) of the Narnia *books.*

Mains, David and Karen. *Tales of the Resistance*. Lamplighter Publishing, 1986.
This is part of the Kingdom Tales *trilogy, but no spoilers here. It's an obvious allegorical story and quite clear both who the Christ figure is and what will happen to him.*

McKelvey, Douglas Kaine. *Every Moment Holy Vol. II: Death, Grief, and Hope*. Rabbit Room, 2021.
A collection of liturgies to help us pray and process through the sorrow-filled moments of life.

Peterson, Andrew. *The Warden and the Wolf King*. Rabbit Room, 2014. *This is the fourth and final book in* The Wingfeather Saga, *and the chapter recommended is a spoiler. Read at your own risk if you haven't already read the books. Skip the reading if you want to get the full experience of this beautiful story.* The Wingfeather Saga *is a highly popular series of four books from Andrew Peterson set in a richly built fantasy world. The books tend towards darker humor and darker themes but can be read and enjoyed by young children. You know your own kids best, so if you're concerned about the content being too heavy, pre-read the books to see what you think.*

Runcie, James. *The Great Passion*. Bloomsbury Publishing, 2022. *This historical/biographical fiction book is centered on Stefan Silbermann, a 13-year-old boy sent to the St. Thomas school in Leipzig in 1727 where his life intertwines with the school's Cantor, Johann Sebastian Bach. The novel deals with grief, rejection, religion, and Bach in a manner that echoes the music referenced throughout. The themes and characters harmonize, collide, and bring to bear truths we have forgotten, or just can't see in our personal depths of despair. The story draws to a close with the first performance of* St. Matthew Passion. *I highly recommend reading this aloud with older children leading into Lent. There are some coming of age moments that are too raw for young children and a horrific execution scene that you may want to edit out, but for kids old enough it will bring to life not just the oratorio, but the person of Bach.*

Venezia, Mike. "Getting to Know the World's Greatest Composers: Johann Sebastian Bach" Children's Press, 2017. *Another picture book biography of Bach, but this one is a lot meatier. Our girls eat up this series on artists, composers, scientists, and inventors, but they can be hard to find. The brilliance here is the combination of art from the period, detailed biographical information, and cartoon illustrations complete with silly speech and thought bubbles. Those silly cartoons cement the facts into our heads. I say "our" because I'm very much including myself!*

Lent Listening Guide

Week One

My God, if writings may
Convey a Lordship any way
Whither the buyer and seller please;
Let it not thee displease,
If this poor paper do as much as they.

On it my heart doth bleed
As many lines, as there doth need
To pass it self and all it hath to thee,
To which I do agree,
And here present it as my special deed.

—George Herbert in "Obedience"

Shrove Tuesday

Shrove Tuesday has become a day of confession, absolution, and celebration for Christians all over the world. The word "shrove" comes to us from the Middle English *shriven* meaning "make confession." On this day, Christians seek to confess and absolve their sins while feasting on rich ingredients they won't partake of during the Lenten season. It is also when some traditions burn the palm leaves from the previous year's Palm Sunday in preparation for Ash Wednesday.

Our family takes time on Shrove Tuesday to prepare for Ash Wednesday, and to have a little Fat Tuesday fun before the full weight of Lent falls upon us. We've created a delightful mix of the secular and sacred that sets us up well to start the Lenten season.

The Secular

This day is called Fat Tuesday for a somewhat obvious reason. Before the fasting, we feast! Another name for it is Pancake Day, but that's not referencing the American-style pancakes that may come to mind. Think more along the line of chubby crêpes. You can find a delicious recipe for this savory supper time treat in the "Extras" section at the back of this book and then follow it up by trying to make homemade beignets (also in the back). God gave us a world of wonder for our senses, so take some time today to taste and see that God is good!

The Sacred

After supper, but before we fill up on fried dough covered in honey and powdered sugar, we pause. The table is cleared, and everyone turns their silly dials to zero while we put dried leaves in a bowl for burning. It's tradition to use the leaves from the previous year's Palm Sunday to make the ash, but don't get too caught up in following traditions and miss out on today. If those old palms (or any palms) aren't available to you, just make do. Living in the tropics provides our yard with copious amounts of dead coconut palms.

We're easily able to grab one, but by all means, burn whatever plant leaf is available to you in order to have a little bit of ash ready for tomorrow. It takes just a tiny bit.

Once everything is set up and all bodies are settled down, we take time to talk about what's coming; namely, Ash Wednesday, Lent in general, sorrowing, and repenting. We pray together through the liturgy "An Exhortation Making Space to Speak of Dying" found in *Every Moment Holy Volume II: Death, Grief, and Hope*. Currently, this liturgy is freely available on the Rabbit Room website, but if at all possible, try and get *Every Moment Holy Volumes I and II*. These books have enriched our family's prayer life in numerous ways, from memorizing a liturgy to speak into the dark when the kids wake up from nightmares to stopping arguments with a quick recitation of the liturgy for fleeting irritations. I recommend using two liturgies during Lent and Easter, both available online right now and both found in Volume II.[18]

The first time we prayed through "An Exhortation Making Space to Speak of Dying" with our 9-, 7-, and 3-year old daughters, it opened wide a door for them to ask simmering and thus far unspoken questions. We were able to openly discuss fear of our own deaths, fear of losing loved ones (at the time all our hearts were still raw from the sudden death of a cherished friend), and fear of the unknown. Lent is about the darker things of this world and in our hearts. This liturgy provides a gentle and reassuring way for your children to start grappling with those things.

Once the discussion comes to a natural close, we (carefully) burn the leaves preparing the ash for tomorrow. The end of our sacred time comes by listening to the modern-day hymn "Come Behold the Wondrous Mystery" sung by The Gray Havens. They did not write the hymn, but their version is vocally crisp, allowing the words to penetrate your soul without distraction.

The Secular

Now we jump back into silly mode eating beignets and playing games! It's a delicate balance of levity and solemnity tonight, paving the way for the storied road ahead.

Day 1—Ash Wednesday
(7 minutes)

The opening of *St. Matthew Passion* is dramatic and compelling. It feels like we're entering into the middle of the story, not at a clear beginning. The depth of drama is paradigmatic of the Baroque zeitgeist. There are two adult choirs, two orchestras, and a boys' choir all intertwining with one another and inviting us into the drama already unfolding. The adult choirs represent the Daughters of Zion and the Faithful; the Daughters of Zion personify Jerusalem through Choir 1 while the Faithful personify Christian faith through Choir 2.[19] As the adult choirs are stunning us with their call and response, the boys' choir enters singing a chorale that blankets the more frenetic dialogue occurring between the Daughters and the Faithful.

Imagine sitting in the St. Thomas Church in Leipzig with two adult choirs positioned about thirty meters (100 feet) opposite each other, their strong voices reverberating in the vaulted ceilings. It would have been magnificent. We can't come close to that experience with our piddly speakers, but as Shakespeare pleads with his audience in the prologue to *Henry V*, so I'm pleading with you: "Let us, ciphers to this great account, on your imaginary forces work."[20] Allow the story Picander is unfolding in the libretto to intertwine with Bach's phenomenal music in a manner that transports your imagination to the reverberating sanctuary your speakers just won't live up to, but your soul very much can.

There is no scripture directly associated with this number but reading through Matthew 25 gives the coming story its legs. These are the three final teachings of Jesus Matthew chooses to highlight just before the traumatic events that unfold in Matthew 26 and 27. These teachings unequivocally communicate what actions are expected of someone who follows Jesus: be prepared for his return, work diligently at your ministry, and care for the oppressed. Full stop. Challenge your children to move through the day remembering that the last teaching we have from Jesus before the arrest and crucifixion are all about dying to yourself. So intentionally walk in sacrificial love today allowing the ash cross (see next page) on your foreheads to be a constant reminder of Jesus's clear directive.

The Great Passion

Scripture Reading

Matthew 25

Listening

Gardiner's recording: Track 1 (6:59)

Libretto

Track 1 (6:59)
No. 1 Chorus
(BWV No. 1)

Kommt, ihr Töchter, helft mir klagen!
Sehet! Wen? Den Bräutigam.
Seht ihn! Wie? Als wie ein Lamm!
Sehet! Was? Seht die Geduld.
Seht! Wohin? Auf unsre Schuld.

Sehet ihn aus Lieb und Huld
Holz zum Kreuze selber tragen!

Come, you daughters, help me wail!
Look! Whom? The Bridegroom.
Look at him! How? He's like a lamb!
Look! What? See his patience.
Look! Where? At our guilt.

See him, in love and grace
He's carrying the wooden cross himself!

Chorale

O Lamm Gottes, unschuldig	O sinless Lamb of God
Am Stamm des Kreuzes geschlachtet,	Slaughtered beneath the cross,
Allzeit erfunden geduldig,	Always patient,
Wiewohl du warest verachtet.	Even though you were disdained.
All Sünd hast du getragen,	You carried all our sin,
Sonst müßten wir verzagen.	Or else we would have to despair.
Erbarm dich unser, o Jesu!	Have mercy on us, O Jesus!

Poem

Ash Wednesday

CHRISTINA ROSSETTI

My God, my God, have mercy on my sin,
For it is great; and if I should begin
To tell it all, the day would be too small
To tell it in.

My God, Thou wilt have mercy on my sin
For Thy Love's sake; yea, if I should begin
To tell Thee all, the day would be too small
To tell it in.

Mark your children's foreheads with the sign of the cross using the ash you made yesterday. This is a stark reminder that we come from ashes and to ashes we will return. It also signifies mourning our sinful state; Lent is penitence. Remind your children to die to self and live out Christ's last teachings.

The Lenten season, a time when believers all over the world will fast, worship, and reflect on our deep need for Jesus's sacrifice, has officially begun.

Day 2—Thursday
(9 minutes)

Now we enter the clear start of the narrative with the Evangelist. He's going to walk us through the story as the primary narrator.

Today you'll experience everything this oratorio has to offer: character solos, the choir in full form, a chorale, and response numbers including an accompagnato recitative or "accompanied recitative" and an aria. The oratorio has a handful of main characters we'll hear from repeatedly: the Evangelist, Jesus, and Peter. Judas, two High Priests, Pontius Pilate, Pilate's wife, two false witnesses, and two maids are also named parts. These "character" parts are all either recitatives or arias, sometimes in duet or sometimes accompanied by orchestration. The false witnesses come from Choir 2 while all the rest of the character soloists come from Choir 1.[21] Bach needed two choirs for his sound drama. The crowds occasionally have a dialogue, much like what you heard yesterday in the discussion between the Daughters of Zion and the Faithful. You'll hear the choirs again today as the priests discuss when and how they'll entrap Jesus and when the disciples protest the "wasted" perfume. The accompanied recitative reflecting on this part of the story comes from the woman with the perfume. She equates the ointment with her tears and Bach uses the adjoining flute to fill our ears with the sound of dropping water.[22] Listen for that with your children!

Bach uses accompanied recitatives for some of the character parts as well as in reflective pieces. One of the most poignant accompagnato recitatives is found in Jesus's solos. Bach has the entire string section of the first orchestra (remember he wrote this for a double orchestra!) using longer notes to highlight the *Vox Christi* or "words of Christ." This has lovingly been referred to as "Jesus's halo." The only time the halo is absent throughout the oratorio is when Jesus utters his final words, "My God, my God, why have you forsaken me?"[23] The halo will appear with someone else, and it is fun to let your children know that here at the beginning so they can start critically thinking through who might receive the halo strings later on. Compositional choices like this bring the libretto to life through the music and demonstrate why this particular oratorio is considered the greatest of the Baroque Era by many scholars.

The Great Passion

Scripture Reading

Matthew 26:1-13

Listening

Gardiner's recording: Track 2 (:36); Track 3 (:38); Track 4 (2:52); Track 5 (:52); Track 6 (4:14)

Libretto

Track 2 (:36)
No. 2 Recitative (Evangelist and Jesus)
(BWV No. 2)

Evangelist

Da Jesus diese Rede volendet hatte, sprach er zu seinen Jüngern:	When Jesus had finished all these teachings, he said to his disciples:

Jesus

Ihr wisest, dass nach zweien Tagen Ostern wird, und des Menschen Sohn wird überantwortet werden, dass er gekreuziget werde.	You know, it's going to be the Passover and the Son of Man will be turned in to be crucified.

Track 3 (:38)
No. 3 Chorale
(BWV No. 3)

Herzliebster Jesu, was hast du verbrochen,
Dass man ein solch scharf Urteil hat gesprochen?
Was ist die Schuld, in was für Missetaten
Bist du geraten?

Beloved Jesus, what have you done wrong,
That they have given you such a harsh sentence?
What are you guilty of, what sorts of bad behavior
have you fallen into?

Track 4 (2:52)
No. 4a-4e Recitative (Evangelist, Chorus, and Jesus)
(BWV Nos. 4-8)

Evangelist

Da versammleten sich die Hohepriester und Schriftgelehrten und die Ältesten im Volk in dem Palast des Hohepriesters, der da hieß Kaiphas, und hielten Rat, wie sie Jesum mit Listen griffen und töteten. Sie sprachen aber:

The high priests and scribes got together alongside the elders of the people in the High Priest Caiphas's palace. They discussed how they might secretly accomplish Jesus's capture and execution. But they said:

Chorus

Ja nicht auf das Fest, auf dass nicht ein Aufruhr werde im Volk.

Not at the time of the celebrations in case it causes an uproar among the people.

Evangelist

Da nun Jesus war zu Bethanien, im Hause Simonis des Aussätzigen,

When Jesus visited Bethany in the house of the leper Simon,

trat zu ihm ein Weib, die hatte ein Glas mit köstlichem Wasser und goß es auf sein Haupt, da er zu Tische saß.
Da das seine Jünger sahen wurden sie unwillig und sprachen:

a woman came to him with a precious jar of perfume. She poured it on his head while he sat at the table.
When the disciples saw it, they became frustrated and said:

Chorus

Wozu dienet dieser Unrat? Dieses Wasser hätte mögen teuer verkauft und den Armen gegeben werden.

To what end are you pouring out this good perfume? It might have sold for lot of money that could have been given to the poor.

Evangelist

Da das Jesus merkete, sprach er zu ihnen:

When Jesus heard them saying this, he said:

Jesus

Was bekümmert ihr das Weib? Sie hat ein gut Werk an mir getan. Ihr habet allezeit Armen bei euch, mich aber habt ihr nicht allezeit.
Dass sie dies Wasser hat auf meinen Leib gegossen, hat sie getan, dass man mich begraben wird.
Wahrlich, ich sage euch: Wo dies Evangelium geprediget wird in der ganzen Welt, da wird man auch sagen zu ihrem Gedächtnis, was sie getan hat.

Why are you bothering this woman? She has done a good thing to me! You'll always have the poor with you, but you won't always have me. She poured this perfume on my body because I'm to be buried.

Truly I say to you, the story of what she's done for me in this moment will be told in her memory wherever the gospel is preached.

Track 5 (:52)
No. 5 Accompanied Recitative (Alto)
(BWV No. 9)

Du lieber Heiland du,	Beloved Savior,
Wenn deine Jünger töricht straiten,	While your disciples argue foolishly,
Dass dieses fromme Weib	This faithful woman
Mit Salben deinen Leib	Rubs your body with ointment
Zum Grabe will bereiten,	To make it ready to bury,
So lasse mir inzwischen zu,	Oh, in the meantime let me,
Von meiner Augen Tränen- flüssen	From my eyes' flood of tears
Ein Wasser auf dein Haupt zu gießen!	Pour as water on your head!

Track 6 (4:14)
No. 6 Aria (Alto)
(BWV No. 10)

Buß' und Reu'	Repentance and remorse
Knirscht das Sündenherz entzwei,	Split the sinful heart in two,
Dass die Tropten meiner Zähren	So that the drops of my tears
Angenehme Spezerei,	A most comforting rich balm,
Treuer Jesu, dir geb	Precious Jesus, I give them to you.

Day 3—Friday
(5 ½ minutes)

Believe it or not, Judas was once a baby with a mother. He grew into a toddler and enjoyed the golden years of childhood. Bach intentionally paints a picture of Judas's everyman persona throughout the oratorio. Judas actually is "every man" in that any one of us could be him. Bach starts this line of thinking in today's aria by combining motherly imagery with a condemnation of Judas's pursuit of money.

It's jarring to take Judas out of his firmly held position as villain-without-a-backstory and remember that he was a human, just like the rest of us, but Bach is right. There go we, but for the grace of God.

The Great Passion

Scripture Reading

Matthew 26:14-16

Listening

Gardiner's recording: Track 7 (:35); Track 8 (4:43)

Libretto

Track 7 (:35)
No. 7 Recitative (Evangelist and Judas)
(BWV No. 11)

Evangelist

Da ging hin der Zwölfen einer, mit Namen Judas Ischarioth, zu den Hohepriestern und sprach:	Then one of the twelve, Judas Iscariot, went to see the high priests and said:

49

Judas

Was wollt ihr mir geben? Ich will ihn euch verraten.

What will you give me? I'm willing to betray him for you.

Evangelist

Und sie boten ihm dreißig Silberlinge. Und von dem an suchte er Gelegenheit, dass er ihn verriete.

They offered him thirty pieces of silver, and from that moment on he looked for a chance to betray Jesus.

Track 8 (4:43)
No. 8 Aria (Soprano)
(BWV No. 12)

Blute nur, du liebes Herz!
Ach! Ein Kind, das du erzogen,
Das an deiner Brust gesogen,
Droht den Pfleger zu ermorden,
Denn es ist zur Schlange worden.

Bleed on, precious heart!
Oh, a child you raised,
That nursed at your breast,
Threatens to murder,

Because it has become a snake.

Day 4—Saturday

Today is a feast of options! Don't be overwhelmed by it all, the intent is to get some ideas and choose one or two for your situation to draw Lent into the weekend.

Activities

Reading Options

Becoming Bach by Tom Leonard

Getting to Know the World's Greatest Composers: Johann Sebastian Bach by Mike Venezia

Getting to Know the World's Greatest Composers: Leonard Bernstein by Mike Venezia

Media Options

Superbook, Season 1, Episode 10 ("The Last Supper")

The Chosen, Season 1, Episode 7 ("Invitations")

For younger children, *Superbook* is excellent at bringing the Bible to life. If you can access this show through streaming or online services, find Season 1, Episode 10 ("The Last Supper") to view today. This presents only part of the story and will leave you hanging on for the next episode. Feel free to forge ahead, but there is space for viewing the next episode on Day 39 when we head into Holy Week.

Superbook probably isn't a great option for older children. For them I would recommend watching Season 1, Episode 7 ("Invitations") from *The Chosen*. This episode harkens back to the Old Testament story of Moses and the bronze serpent, clearly pointing to Christ on the cross. As a part of your viewing, you can go back and read Numbers 21:6-9 and focus on how the story of Jesus and his redemptive death is threaded throughout Scripture.

A final option today is to read aloud any combination of the following throughout the day: *Getting to Know the World's Greatest Composers: Johann Sebastian Bach* by Mike Venezia; *Getting to Know the World's Greatest Composers: Leonard Bernstein* by Mike Venezia; or the picture book *Becoming Bach* by Tom Leonard. Clearly these are leaning more into teaching your children music history and are less about Lent itself. We sprinkle these throughout the day as impromptu read-alouds to fortify what our children are learning about music history throughout the Lenten weeks.

Sunday

S pend your time together recognizing that Lent is a journey we're just beginning. It will ultimately lead to the foot of the cross and the doorstep of Easter's bright morning. Lent will take weeks of discipline and discomfort (if you're fasting), but this is meant to be a microcosm of our walk through life following Jesus, and an opportunity for us to actively participate in the all-important practice of *remembering*. Today's poem does not speak directly to the Lent journey, but instead to the pilgrimage of Christians throughout their faith life. Some believe this poem was the inspiration for *The Pilgrim's Progress* by John Bunyan, and certainly you can see the similarities. You can find more insight about it in Malcolm Guite's *The Word in the Wilderness*.

Poem

The Pilgrimage
George Herbert

I travell'd on, seeing the hill, where lay
　　My expectation.
　A long it was a weary way.
　The gloomy cave of Desperation
I left on th'one, and on the other side
　　The Rock of Pride.

And so I Came to Fancy's meadow strow'd
　　With many a flower:
　Fair would I here have made abode,
　But I was quicken'd by my houre.
So to Care's copse I came, and there got through
　　With much ado.

That led me to the wild of Passion, which
　　　　Some call the wold;
　　　A wasted place, but sometimes rich.
　　　Here I was robb'd of all my gold,
Save one good Angel, which a friend had ti'd
　　　　Close to my side.

At length I got unto the gladsome hill,
　　　　Where lay my hope,
　　　Where lay my heart; and climbing still,
　　　When I had gain'd the brow and top,
A lake of brackish waters on the ground
　　　　Was all I found.

With that abash'd and struck with many a sting
　　　　Of swarming fears,
　　　I fell, and cry'd, Alas my King;
　　　Can both the way and end be tears?
Yet taking heart I rose, and then perceiv'd
　　　　I was deceiv'd:

My hill was further: so I flung away,
　　　　Yet heard a crie
　　　Just as I went, None goes that way
　　　And lives: If that be all, said I,
After so foul a journey death is fair,
　　　　And but a chair.

Week Two

If that hereafter Pleasure
Cavil, and claim her part and measure,
As if this passed with a reservation,
Or some such words in fashion;
I here exclude the wrangler from thy treasure.

O let thy sacred will
All thy delight in me fulfill!
Let me not think an action mine own way,
But as thy love shall sway,
Resigning up the rudder to thy skill.

—George Herbert in "Obedience"

Day 5—Monday
(2½ minutes)

Bach immediately continues to push us into the story as active players rather than passive consumers. On Friday we took time to reflect on Judas as a man any one of us could be. Today we step into the role of the disciples during the Passover supper when they find out one of them will betray Jesus. Bach gives us their response to this revelation through the chorus's panicked repetition of "Lord, is it I?" eleven times over. That number isn't random. Really nothing in this oratorio is random. Bach chooses eleven to represent each disciple actually reacting that way. Obviously, Judas Iscariot has a different thought process, and Bach knew this. He intentionally leaves Judas out.[24] The manner in which the chorus echoes back and forth and all over the place with this short, repeated line works on our own hearts in a strange way. By the end we're asking ourselves not if it's one of them, but is it, in fact, I?

Bach gives us our answer with the scene-ending chorale. Yes, it is all of us. It is I, sitting in the congregation listening to this 1,700 years later in St. Thomas Church, Leipzig. It is I, sitting in the living room listening to this another 300 years after Bach. We all participate in the betrayal and crucifixion of our Lord, and it stuns.

This is a small but brilliant musical number that adds to the depth of Bach's storytelling abilities and to the drama of the overall piece.

The Great Passion

Scripture Reading

Matthew 26:17-22

Listening

Gardiner's recording: Track 9 (1:54); Track 10 (:43)

Libretto

Track 9 (1:54)
No. 9a-9e Recitative (Evangelist, Chorus, and Jesus)
(BWV Nos. 13-15)

Evangelist

Aber am ersten Tage der süßen Brote traten die Jünger zu Jesu und sprachen zu ihm:

On the first day of Unleavened Bread the disciples came to Jesus and said:

Chorus

Wo willst du, dass wir dir bereiten, das Osterlamm zu essen?

Where do you want us to prepare to have the Passover supper?

Evangelist

Er sprach:

He said:

Jesus

Gehet hin in die Stadt zu einem und sprecht zu ihm: Der Meister laßt dir sagen: Meine Zeit ist hier, ich will bei dir die Ostern halten mit meinen Jüngern.

Go into the town and say to a man there: The Master sends you a message: My time is here, I want to keep Passover with my disciples in your house.

Evangelist

Und die Jünger täten, wie ihnen Jesus befohlen hatte, und bereiteten das Osterlamm. Und am Abend satzte er sich zu Tische mit den Zwölfen. Und da sie aßen, sprach er:

The disciples did as Jesus asked and prepared the Passover lamb. In the evening, Jesus sat down with the twelve. While they ate he said:

Jesus

Wahrlich, ich sage euch: Einer unter euch wird mich verraten.

Truly I say to you, one of you will betray me.

Evangelist

Und sie wurden sehr betrübt und huben an, ein jeglicher unter ihnen, und sagten zu ihm:	They were distressed and began to say to Jesus in turn:

Chorus

Herr, bin ich's?	Lord, is it I?

Track 10 (:43)
No. 10 Chorale
(BWV No. 16)

Ich bin's, ich sollte büßen,	It is I, I should pay the price,
An Händen und an Füßen	My hands and feet
Gebunden in der Höll.	Tied up in Hell.
Die Geißeln und die Banden	The whip and the chains
Und was du ausgestanden,	And all that you endured,
Das hat verdienet meine Seel.	Is what my soul has earned.

Day 6—Tuesday
(4 minutes)

We're watching more remarkable moments unfold during the Passover supper in Scene 5. After the narrative, you'll hear the reflective recitative today and the reflective aria tomorrow. The scene is focused on two major events: the outward acknowledgement by Jesus of Judas's intent to betray him and Jesus giving the instructions for observing the Eucharist (Lord's Supper or Holy Communion).

The act of communion is central to the Christian faith. It is a remembrance, a fellowship, an outward display of belief, and, perhaps most importantly, a simple act of obedience. Jesus commands us to do this, so we do it. Bach recognizes that the inception of the Lord's Supper is a moment worth marking. He does this with two reflective pieces sung on behalf of Christendom. The word "eucharist" means thanksgiving, and that is what we do as we meditate on Communion in No. 12 (BWV No. 18) today, and No. 13 (BWV No. 19) tomorrow.

The Great Passion

Scripture Reading

Matthew 26:23-29

Listening

Gardiner's recording: Track 11 (2:34); Track 12 (1:18);

Libretto

Track 11 (2:34)
No. 11 Recitative (Evangelist, Jesus, and Judas)
(BWV No. 17)

Evangelist

Er antwortete und sprache:

He answered and said:

Jesus

Der mit der Hand mit mir in die Schüssel tauchet, der wird mich verraten. Des Menschen Sohn gehet zwar dahin, wie von ihm geschrieben stehet; doch wehe dem Menschen, durch welchen des Menschen Sohn verraten wird!
Es wäre ihm besser, dass derselbige Mensch noch nie geboren wäre.

He whose hand dips with me will betray me. The Son of Man will go as it has been prophesied, but great tragedy waits for the man who betrayed him.

It would be better for him if he had never been born.

Evangelist

Da antwortete Judas, der ihn verriet, und sprach:

Judas, the one who would betray him, answered and said:

Judas

Bin ich's, Rabbi?

Is it I, Teacher?

Evangelist

Er sprach zu ihm:

He said to him:

Jesus

Du sagest's.

As you say.

Evangelist

Da sie aber aßen, nahm Jesus das Brot, dankete und brach's und gab's den Jüngern und sprach:

While they were eating, Jesus took the bread, gave thanks, and broke it. He gave it to his disciples saying:

Jesus

Nehmet, esset, das ist mein Leib.

Take and eat, this is my Body.

Evangelist

| Und er nahm den Kelch und dankete, gab ihnen den und sprach: | Then he took the cup, gave thanks, and gave it to them saying: |

Jesus

Trinket alle daraus; das ist mein Blut des neuen Testaments, welches vergossen wird für viele zur Vergebung der Sünden.

All of you, drink this. It is my blood of the New Testament, poured out here for the forgiveness of the sins of many.

Ich sage euch: Ich werde von nun an nicht mehr von diesem Gewächs des Weinstocks trinken bis an den Tag, da ich's neu trinken werde mit euch in meines Vaters Reich.

I tell you, I won't drink wine from this moment until the day I'll drink it with you in my Father's kingdom.

Track 12 (1:18)
No. 12 Recitative (Soprano)
(BWV No. 18)

Wiewohl mein Herz in Tränen schwimmt,
Dass Jesus von mir Abschied nimmt,
So macht mich doch sein Testament erfreut:
Sein Fleisch und Blut, o Kostbarkeit,
Vermacht er mir in meine Hände.
Wie er es auf der Welt mit denen Seinen
Nicht böse können meinen,
So liebt er sie bis an das Ende.

Even though my heart swims in tears,
Because Jesus is leaving us,

Even so his promise makes me glad:
His body and blood, O preciousness,
He gives into my hands.

To his own people here on earth
He could not mean ill,
So he loved them till the end.

Day 7—Wednesday
(3 minutes)

This is the scene-ending aria that gives us more time to reflect on the import of the Lord's Supper.

The Great Passion

Scripture Reading

No reading

Listening

Gardiner's recording: Track 13 (2:56)

Libretto

Track 13 (2:56)
No. 13 Aria (Soprano)
(BWV No. 19)

Ich will dir mein Herze schenken,	I will give my heart to you,
Senke dich, mein Heil, hinein!	Sink into it, my Salvation!
Ich will mich in dir versenken;	I will immerse myself in you;
Ist dir gleich die Welt zu klein, Ei,	Though the world is too small for you,
so sollst du mir allein	Ah, then for me alone you will
Mehr als Welt und Himmel sein.	Be more than world and heaven.

Day 8—Thursday
(2 minutes)

Prepare yourselves! There is a wealth of symbolism and emotion brimming over in today's recitative and chorale. After meditating on the Eucharist during the previous two numbers, Bach pulls us directly back into the story by bringing it alive in the instrumentation. He then follows the brief narrative with a deeply symbolic chorale.

Take a moment to review where we're at in the story. The disciples have just participated in the first Holy Communion and are finishing their time in the upper room. Before anything else happens, we have to get out of that room and onto the Mount of Olives—an event that will be bodily represented in the sound drama. The Evangelist's voice rises as they go, enlivening our imaginations to the quick journey. Once there, Jesus prophesies to the disciples of their upcoming scattering.[25]

Remember that every time the bass soloist from Choir 1 sings as Jesus, he is accompanied by the strings or "Jesus's halo." Occasionally, Bach uses those strings to effectively paint a mental picture of the action or to express a certain emotion; here we get a very vivid picture. When Jesus mentions the scattering sheep, the strings become frenzied, immediately bringing to mind sheep running to and fro in a panic.[26] This brief moment of chaos is brought into calm order via the chorale.

You will probably recognize the melody of the chorale as "O Sacred Head, Now Wounded," a hymn still popular today. It is used directly after the scattering of the sheep prophesy as a reminder of our surety in Jesus. We will scatter, but we have a good Shepherd who will not so easily abandon his sheep.

As I hope you've caught on by now, everything in this oratorio means something. We're just barely scratching the surface. This chorale shows up five intentional times to both weave its familiar strain from beginning to end and to symbolize the five wounds of Christ: his scourging, the crown of thorns, the nails in his hands, his feet, and his pierced side.[27] In the chorale we are given the opportunity to pause and contemplate ourselves running from Jesus when following him becomes utterly terrifying. We pause and see the boundless hope he offers; we scatter, but he will gather.

The Great Passion

Scripture Reading

Matthew 26:30-32

Listening

Gardiner's recording: Track 14 (:53); Track 15 (:51)

Libretto

Track 14 (:53)
No. 14 Recitative (Evangelist and Jesus)
(BWV No. 20)

Evangelist

Und da sie den Lobgesang gesprochen hatten, gingen sie hinaus an den Ölberg. Da sprach Jesus zu ihnen:

After reciting the song of praise, they went to the Mount of Olives. There Jesus said to them:

Jesus

In dieser Nacht werdet ihr euch alle ärgern an mir. Denn es stehet geschrieben: Ich werde den Hirten schlagen, und die Schafe der Herde werden sich zerstreuen. Wenn ich aber auferstehe, will ich vor euch hingehen in Galiläam.

Tonight you'll be offended because of me. Like it says in the scripture: I will strike down the shepherd and the sheep will be alone and will scatter. When I am risen, I will go ahead of you into Galilee.

Track 15 (:51)
No. 15 Chorale
(BWV No. 21)

Erkenne mich, mein Hüter,	Know me, my defender,
Mein Hirte, nimm mich an!	My shepherd, take me to you.
Von dir, Quell aller Güter,	You are the source of all good-ness,
Ist mir viel Guts getan.	Many good things have hap-pened to me.
Dein Mund hat mich gelabet	Your mouth has given me refreshment
Mit Milch und süßer Kost,	With milk and sweets,
Dein Geist hat mich begabet	Your spirit has blessed me
Mit mancher Himmelslust.	With many divine desires.

Day 9—Friday

(2 minutes)

The recitative in No. 16 (BWV No. 22) is between the Evangelist, hopeful Peter, and a patient Jesus. Peter says what we all hope to be true of ourselves. He wants to stand by Jesus no matter what comes.

The chorale becomes a voice for Peter's heart desire and gives words to the longing in our own faith lives. It is the second time Bach uses "O Sacred Head, Now Wounded," and it represents Peter's declaration and vow. He wants to prove his love for his Teacher through ministering to him in his darkest hour, and standing by him.

It's a sorrow-filled point in the story because we know Peter won't fulfill his promise and Jesus knows this too. Peter won't be there to soothe him during his torture or partake with him in the crucifixion (at that point in Peter's life, at least). Peter's fear ultimately overcomes him. Will we be like Peter, or will we be full of faithful courage?

Don't end the week on this note. Remind your children of the hope on the other side of this bit of the story. Jesus knew that Peter would fail, but he still loved him, died for him, and freely forgave him. At the end of his life, Peter is given the opportunity to redo this moment and he does stand faithfully, even unto the cross.

The Great Passion

Scripture Reading

Matthew 26:33-35

Listening

Gardiner's *recording*: Track 16 (:52); Track 17 (:52)

Libretto

Track 16 (:52)
No. 16 Recitative (Evangelist, Peter, and Jesus)
(BWV No. 22)

Evangelist

Petrus aber antwortete und sprach zu ihm:

Peter answered and said to him:

Peter

Wenn sie auch alle sich an dir ärgerten, so will ich doch mich nimmermehr ärgern.

Even though the others will be offended by you, I'll never feel that way.

Evangelist

Jesus sprach zu ihm:

Jesus responded:

Jesus

Wahrlich, ich sage dir: In dieser Nacht, ehe der Hahn krähet, wirst du mich dreimal verleugnen.

Hear me! This very night before the cock crows three times, you'll deny me three times.

Evangelist

Petrus sprach zu ihm:

Peter said to him:

Peter

Und wenn ich mit dir sterben müßte, so will ich dich nicht verleugnen.

Even if I have to die with you, I won't deny you.

Evangelist

Desgleichen sagten auch alle Jünger.

All the other disciples agreed.

Track 17 (:52)
No. 17 Chorale
(BWV No. 23)

Ich will hier bei dir stehen;	I will stand beside you;
Verachte mich doch nicht!	Don't scorn me!
Von dir will ich nicht gehen,	I won't depart from you,
Wenn dir dein Herze bricht.	Even if your heart is breaking.
Wenn dein Herz wird erblassen	When your heart grows afraid
Im letzten Todesstoß,	In the last throes of death,
Asldenn will ich dich fassen	Then I will hold you
In meinen Arm und Schoß.	In my arms and lap.

Day 10—Saturday

Reading

The Lion, the Witch and the Wardrobe by C. S. Lewis, chapter 14

Listening

Sarah Sparks's song "Blood for Blood" from the album *Into the Lantern Waste*

Read aloud chapter 14 from *The Lion, the Witch and the Wardrobe* by C.S. Lewis. You're diving right into the thick of the story witnessing Aslan's sacrificial death at the hands of the witch on the Stone Table. It may be interesting to note that even though many readers categorize the Narnia stories as an allegory, Lewis never did. He wrote them as parallel fantasies with the germ idea being the question: How would God manifest himself if other worlds or lands existed?[28] On Earth, he is a man. In Narnia, he is a lion. Jesus very much exists already in this universe, so Aslan can't be a stand-in for him symbolically. Aslan is Jesus, Jesus is Aslan. They're just in different worlds.

When you've finished reading, listen to the song "Blood for Blood" by Sarah Sparks. This comes from *Into the Lantern Waste*, a concept album in which each song is dedicated to a different aspect or character from the Narnia series. It's a stunning work that I highly recommend listening to in its entirety with your Narnia loving children. This song is focused on the character of Edmund as he processes what Aslan has done on his behalf.

Sunday

I f you are choosing to fast in some manner during this Lenten season, you may find that even this early your children are flagging, or perhaps you yourself are finding it hard to stay true to your chosen abstinence. It's important that we understand why we fast in order to guard the act from becoming a legalistic action, or worse, a matter of pride. When we're grounded in the whys of any spiritual discipline we practice, then, and only then, can we fully communicate its import to our children. So take a moment today to review about Lenten fasting ("What is Lent?" pages 17-20).

Remember that the forty days of Lent connect us to the forty days Jesus fasted in the wilderness (Matthew 4:1-2). Here are some verses to study in reference to fasting: 1 Samuel 7:3-6, 1 Kings 19:4-8, Ezra 8:21-23, Esther 4:16, Daniel 1:8-21, Matthew 6:16-18, John 6:35, Acts 9:9, and Acts 14:23. This is a good place to start digging in and planting roots for incorporating fasting into your family culture. After you've done some Scriptural studying, read the following poem to give poetic flight to our reasons for fasting.

It's useful to know that the poem was written during a volatile time in English history as Protestants and Catholics vied for power through the monarchy. George Herbert wrestled intellectually with a deep disagreement in the Protestant Church as to whether the Liturgical Calendar, long associated with the Roman Catholic Church, should even be observed.

That debate is not over. There are still many people who believe that the Church Calendar is laying burdens on believers to practice in ways not laid out in the Bible. Herbert believed the Bible teaches quite a lot about spiritual discipline, particularly fasting. He also agreed that anything like the Liturgical Calendar becomes problematic when it is performative.

This poem wrestles through the two extreme responses, ultimately landing on an earnest desire to practice fasting and Lent as an outpouring of deep devotion through service to others. His conclusions are precisely why my low-church Protestant family decided to observe Lent and lean into the Church Calendar to fortify our faith.

As a sidenote, Herbert was a contemporary of Shakespeare living from 1593-1633 and there is some older language in this poem. Here are two such words defined according to the Oxford English Dictionary, so they won't cause stumbling blocks for you or your kids: *sluttish*—unclean, dirty, grimy, untidy; *rheums*—watery matter from nose or eyes.

Poem

Lent
GEORGE HERBERT

Welcome dear feast of Lent; who loves not thee,
He loves not Temperance, or Authority;
            But compos'd of passion.
The Scriptures bid us fast; the Church says, now:
Give to thy Mother, what thou wouldst allow
            To ev'ry Corporation.

The humble soul compos'd of love and fear
Begins at home, and lays the burden there,
            When doctrines disagree.
He says, in things which use hath justly got,
I am a scandal to the Church, and not
            The Church is so to me.

True Christians should be glad of an occasion
To use their temperance, seeking no evasion,
            When good is seasonable;
Unless Authority, which should increase
The obligation in us, make it less
            And Power itself disable.

Besides the cleanness of sweet abstinence,
Quick thoughts and motions at a small expense,
        A face not fearing light:
Whereas in fulness there are sluttish fumes,
Sour exhalations, and dishonest rheums,
        Revenging the delight.

Then those same pendant profits, which the spring
And Easter intimate, enlarge the thing,
        And goodness of the deed.
Neither ought other men's abuse of Lent
Spoil the good use; lest by that argument
        We forfeit all our Creed.

It's true, we cannot reach Christ's forti'th day;
Yet to go part of that religious way,
        Is better than to rest;
We cannot reach our Saviour's purity;
Yet are we bid, Be holy ev'n as he.
        In both let's do our best.

Who goeth in the way which Christ hath gone,
Is much more sure to meet with him, than one
        That travelleth by-ways:
Perhaps my God, though he be far before,
May turn and take me by the hand, and more:
        May strengthen my decays.

Yet Lord instruct us to improve our fast
By starving sin and taking such repast,
        As may our faults control:
That ev'ry man may revel at his door,
Not in his parlour; banqueting the poor,
        And among those his soul.

Week Three

Lord, what is man to thee,
That thou shouldst mind a rotten tree?
Yet since thou canst not choose but see my actions;
So great are thy perfections,
Thou mayst as well my actions guide, as see.

—GEORGE HERBERT IN "OBEDIENCE"

Day 11—Monday
(3½ minutes)

Bach propels us into the Garden of Gethsemane where we begin to swim the dark waters of Jesus's sorrowing. The narrative recitative is followed by a reflective recitative and aria helping us to process what we're silently witnessing. Both numbers are a call and response between the tenor soloist in Choir 1 and the chorus sung by Choir 2. The soloist and choir are stationed far from one another to communicate visually that this is a conversation.[29] We will listen to the narrative and reflective recitatives today, the aria tomorrow.

Scripture Reading

Matthew 26:36-38

Listening

Gardiner's recording: Track 18 (1:28); Track 19 (1:58)

Libretto

Track 18 (1:28)
No. 18 Recitative (Evangelist and Jesus)
(BWV No. 24)

Evangelist

Da kam Jesus mit ihnen zu einem Hofe, der hieß Gethsemane, und sprach zu seinen Jüngern:

Jesus and his disciples went to the Garden of Gethsemane and he said to them:

Jesus

Setzet euch hie, bis dass ich dort hingehe und bete.

Sit here while I go over there to pray.

Evangelist

Und nahm zu sich Petrum und die zween Söhne Zebedäi und fing an zu trauern und zu zagen. Da sprach Jesus zu ihnen:

Taking Peter and the two sons of Zebedee with him, he began to mourn and despair. Then he said to them:

Jesus

Meine Seele ist betrübt bis an den Tod, bleibet hie und wachet mit mir.

My soul is very distressed, to death. Stay here and keep watch with me.

Track 19 (1:58)
No. 19 Recitative (Tenor and Chorus)
(BWV No. 25)

Tenor

O Schmerz!
Hier zittert das gequälte Herz;

O pain!
Here trembles the tortured heart;

Wie sinkt es hin, wie bleicht sein Angesicht!

How it sinks, how pale his face!

Chorus

Was ist die Ursach aller solcher Plagen?

What is the reason for such torments?

Tenor

Der Richter führt ihn vor Gericht.
Da ist kein Trost, kein Helfer nicht.

The judge summons him to court.
There is no hope, no one to help.

Chorus

Ach! Meine Sünden haben dich geschlagen;

Alas, my sins, they are the cause of your pain;

Tenor

Er leidet alle Höllenqualen, er soll vor fremden Raub be-zahlen.

He suffers hell's torments, he's paying for the sins of others.

Chorus

Ich, ach Herr Jesu, habe dies verschuldet
Was du erduldet.

It is me, Jesus, I have caused

What you are now bearing.

Tenor

Ach, könnte meine Liebe dir,
Mein Heil, dein Zittern und dein Zagen
Vermindern oder helfen tragen,
Wie gerne blieb ich hier!

Oh, if only my love for you,
My Savior, your fear and trem-bling
Relieve or help you endure,
How happily I would stay!

Day 12—Tuesday
(5 minutes)

The aria is a powerful follow-up to the reflective recitative, giving voice to the emotions of the moment in dramatic aria style. Why does Jesus endure this heartrending night of prayer? Watching him labor in soul, mind, and body as he contemplates what's coming is bittersweet for us. He suffers to take death away from us. Notice how the instrumentation accompanying the vocals starts off sounding quite alert as the soloist commits to watching with Jesus. The chorus responds softly and almost sleepily as they discuss our sins sleeping. Toward the end there is a subtle shift away from the dichotomy of alertness and sleepiness to soft weeping. Indeed, what we are taking time to remember is inescapably bittersweet.

The Great Passion

Scripture Reading

No reading

Listening

Gardiner's recording: Track 20 (4:57)

Libretto

Track 20 (4:57)
No. 20 Aria (Tenor and Chorus)
(BWV No. 26)

Tenor

Ich will bei meinem Jesu wachen,	I will keep watch with my Jesus,

Chorus

So schlafen unsre Sünden ein.

Then our sins will sleep.

Tenor

Meinen Tod
Bußet seine Seelennot;
Sein Trauren machet mich voll
Freuden.

My death
Is paid for by his anguish;
His sorrow makes me full of
joy.

Chorus

Drum muss uns sein verdien-
stlich Leiden Recht bitter und
doch süße sein.

That's why his praiseworthy
suffering must be bittersweet
for us.

Day 13—Wednesday
(1 ½ minutes)

We know Jesus knew the Tanakh, the Hebrew Scriptures, inside and out. We get to see that in a very real way right here as Bach again slows the story to a snail's pace allowing, and indeed forcing, us to take the time to internalize what's happening. Some scholars refer to this scene as "Agony in the Garden Part 1," which certainly connotes that there will be more agony in the garden coming up.[30] Bach isn't letting us slide through the garden breezily.

In today's portion, Jesus is begging God to release him from the divine plan of redemption. In his agony, fear, and utter humanity, he speaks through the same metaphor found all throughout the Tanakh: the cup of wrath. The cup is due to pour out, but on whom? Here we see Jesus acknowledging that he will bear its full weight, but honestly, he just doesn't want to do it. The reflective recitative homes in on Jesus's relatable human response to the situation while lauding him for being willing to drink the wrath on our behalf, if that is what God ultimately requires.

The Great Passion

Scripture Reading

Matthew 26:39

Listening

Gardiner's recording: Track 21 (:38); Track 22 (:54)

Libretto

Track 21 (:38)
No. 21 Recitative (Evangelist and Jesus)
(BWV No. 27)

Evangelist

Und ging hin ein wenig, fiel nieder auf sein Angesicht und betete und sprach:	He went on for a bit, fell on his face, and having prayed said:

Jesus

Mein Vater, ist's möglich, so gehe dieser Kelch von mir; doch nicht wie ich will, sondern wie du willt.	Father, if it's possible, allow this cup to pass from me; but not my will, rather yours be done.

Track 22 (:54)
No. 22 Recitative (Bass)
(BWV No. 28)

Der Heiland fällt vor seinem Vater nieder;	Jesus falls before his Father;
Dadurch erhebt er sich und alle	In doing so, he raises himself and all the people
Von unserm Falle	From our fall
Hinauf zu Gottes Gnade wieder.	He raises us up to God's grace again.
Er ist bereit,	He is ready,
Den Kelch, des Todes Bitterkeit	The bitter cup of death
Zu trinken,	To drink,
In welchen Sünden dieser Welt	In this cup, the sins of the world
Gegossen sind und hässlich stinken,	Are poured and smell foul,
Weil es dem lieben Gott gefällt.	And he will drink from this cup because it pleases God.

Day 14—Thursday
(4 minutes)

Jesus is vulnerable and scared. He is responding to the monumental task before him in a manner we can all fully understand: he doesn't want to be tortured and to die! What becomes a bit more difficult for our finite human minds to grasp is his ability to follow through, despite the deeply rooted and relatable fears. This is a moment we can stop and recognize that "being a Christian" is more than a label. We can look back to Jesus's teachings and find that being his follower means actively following by *taking up his cross*. It's not warm fuzzies and comfortable living. It can be loss of family, home, and even life itself. Take a moment to talk to your children about the grit of Christianity. Making the choice to follow Jesus is choosing a road of agony alongside him. At the same time, making the choice to follow Jesus is also choosing eternal gain.

Today's scene-ending aria doubles down on the cup metaphor. Picander (remember, he's the librettist and poet responsible for all the bits in the libretto that aren't Biblical narrative or chorales) takes the metaphor a step further here. To follow Jesus, we actually do drink from a bitter cup on this side of eternity, but we are only able to endure its bitterness because Jesus drank first thereby lessening its potency.

The Great Passion

Scripture Reading

No reading

Listening

Gardiner's recording: Track 23 (4:02)

Libretto

Track 23 (4:02)
No. 23 Aria (Bass)
(BWV No. 29)

Gerne will ich mich bequemen,	I will happily,
Kreuz und Becher anzunehmen.	Take up cross and cup.
Trink ich doch dem Heiland nach.	Follow Christ and drink.
Denn sein Mund,	Oh, his mouth,
Der mit Milch und Honig fließet,	Which flows with sweetness,
Hat den Grund	Laid the foundation
Und des Leidens herbe Schmach	And suffering's despair
Durch den ersten Trunk versüßet.	Lessened by drinking it first.

Poem

Read the following poem, another one by George Herbert. He is specifically reflecting on the agony Christ wrestled with in the Garden of Gethsemane and his coming agony on the cross. It dovetails perfectly with how Picander and Bach interpreted Christ's agony in the garden; they all play with metaphors around drinking esoteric ideas (wrath, sin, love).

The Agony
George Herbert

Philosphers have measured mountains,
Fathomed the depths of the seas, of states, and kings,
Walked with a staff to heaven, and traced fountains:
    But there are two vast, special things,
The which to measure it doth more behove,
Yet few there are that sound them: Sin and Love.

    Who would know Sin, let him repair
Unto mount Olivet; there shall he see
A man so wrung with pains, that all his hair,
    His skin, his garments bloody be.
Sin is that press and vice, which forceth pain
To hunt his cruel food through every vein.

    Who knows not Love, let him assay
And taste that juice, which on the cross a pike
Did set again abroach, then let him say
    If ever he did taste the like.
Love is that liquor sweet and most divine,
Which my God feels as blood; but I, as wine.

Day 15—Friday
(2 minutes)

Jesus gets quite stern today during his solo upon discovering the sleeping disciples. Focus your children on how Jesus highlights the importance of prayer in his rebuke. Ask your children to think critically about this. If Peter, who was one of the disciples sleeping, had been diligently praying for and with Jesus, would he have failed in his pledge to stand by Jesus no matter what? Would he have denied Jesus the three times? We'll never know, but it is a chance for your family to grapple with how the story is narrated focusing on a failure to pray faithfully and how this event, that occurred thousands of years ago, can apply to our own lives. It is quite clear all over the Bible that prayer is foundational to our walk with God, but there is much mystery to it. Explore that with your children today and see what thoughts or questions arise.

The Great Passion

Scripture Reading

Matthew 26:40-42

Listening

Gardiner's recording: Track 24 (1:07); Track 25 (:57)

Libretto

Track 24 (1:07)
No. 24 Recitative (Evangelist and Jesus)
(BWV No. 30)

Evangelist

Und er kam zu seinen Jüngern und fand sie schlafend und sprach zu ihnen:

When he came back and found them sleeping he said:

Jesus

Könnet ihr denn nicht eine Stunde mit mir wachen? Wachet und betet, dass ihr nicht in Anfechtung fallet! Der Geist ist willig, aber das Fleisch ist schwach.

Could you not watch with me for just one hour? Watch and pray, or you'll fall into temptation! The spirit is willing, but the flesh is weak.

Evangelist

Zum andernmal ging er hin, betete und sprach:

He went off for a second time to pray and said:

Jesus

Mein Vater, ist's nicht möglich, dass dieser Kelch von mir gehe, ich trinke ihn denn, so geschehe dein Wille.

My Father, if this cup can't pass from me unless I drink it, let your will be done.

Track 25 (:57)
No. 25 Chorale
(BWV No. 31)

Was mein Gott will, das
g'scheh allzeit.
Sein Will, der ist der beste,
Zu helfen den'n er ist bereit,
Die an ihn glauben feste.
Er hilft aus Not, der fromme
Gott,
Und züchtigt mit Maßen.

May God's will always be done.

His will is the best,
He is ready to help those,
Who faithfully believe in him.
And helps them in their time
of need,
And disciplines them within
reason.

Wer Gott vertraut, fest auf ihn
baut,
Den will er nicht verlassen.

Those who confide in God,

Will never be forsaken.

Day 16—Saturday

Reading

Tales of the Resistance by David and Karen Mains, chapter entitled "Traffic Court" (p. 100 "Amanda gasped" to end of chapter)

Listening

Future of Forestry's song "Tears" from the album *Remember*

Today's reading is a small section from a much longer allegorical story set in a fantasy world. This excerpt is directly after the King (Jesus) has been arrested by the Enchanter (Lucifer) and is being put on trial. Amanda and Hero are followers of the King and witnesses to his trial. Later in the guide, you will continue through to the King's execution.

Afterwards, or if you don't have access to the book, listen to "Tears" from *Future of Forestry*. Lent is a time of deep sorrowing and loneliness. When Jesus was in the wilderness for forty days preparing for a hard ministry, he felt lonely. He was fully man and if he had not felt that isolation then the rejection of all Satan's attempts to draw him away from his vigil would have been diminished. But he was fully man and so fully tempted. Our tears are something he gets.

I love this song because it doesn't just lyrically sing away our sorrows, extracting them from our hearts like you would suck poison from a snakebite. It does do that, but it uses the music as much as the words. It's a chance to show your children how even today musicians use instruments alone and without the adornment of words to speak volumes. The self-pity, loneliness, and angst all flow out of me as I hear the pitch and volume steadily increase at the end of the song, taking my hurts on high to the one who can assuage all pain.

Sunday

Read the following prologue to "In Memoriam" by Alfred, Lord Tennyson as found in *The Soul in Paraphrase*.[31] "In Memoriam" is a collection of 131 lyric poems Tennyson wrote as he wrestled with his faith in light of a friend's death. The poems are full of doubt and confusion, but ultimately this prologue is his final statement and was written last. It is a prayer to Jesus.

Poem

Strong Son of God, Immortal Love
ALFRED, LORD TENNYSON

Strong Son of God, immortal Love,
  Whom we, that have not seen thy face,
  By faith, and faith alone, embrace,
Believing where we cannot prove;

Thine are these orbs of light and shade;
  Thou madest life in man and brute;
  Thou madest death; and lo, thy foot
Is on the skull which thou hast made.

Thou wilt not leave us in the dust:
  Thou madest man, he knows not why,
  He thinks he was not made to die;
And thou hast made him; thou art just.

Thou seemest human and divine,
  The highest, holiest manhood, thou.
  Our wills are ours, we know not how,
Our wills are ours, to make them thine.

Our little systems have their day;
        They have their day and cease to be:
        They are but broken lights of thee,
And thou, O Lord, art more than they.

We have but faith: we cannot know;
        For knowledge is of things we see;
        And yet we trust it comes from thee,
A beam in darkness: let it grow.

Let knowledge grow from more to more,
        But more of reverence in us dwell;
        That mind and soul, according well,
May make one music as before,

But vaster. We are fools and slight;
        We mock thee when we do not fear;
        But help thy foolish ones to bear;
Help thy vain worlds to bear thy light.

Forgive what seemed my sin in me,
        What seemed my worth since I began;
        For merit lives from man to man,
And not from man, O Lord, to thee.

Forgive my grief for one removed,
        Thy creature, whom I found so fair.
        I trust he lives in thee, and there
I find him worthier to be loved.

Forgive these wild and wandering cries,
        Confusions of a wasted youth;
        Forgive them where they fail in truth,
And in thy wisdom make me wise.

Week Four

Besides, thy death and blood
Show'd a strange love to all our good:
Thy sorrows were in earnest; no faint proffer,
Or superficial offer
Of what we might not take, or be withstood.

—GEORGE HERBERT IN "OBEDIENCE"

Day 17—Monday
(8 minutes)

After agonizing with Jesus in the garden for a bit, we're now driving relentlessly forward into a highly emotional moment in the oratorio. The narrative recitative moves through quite a lot of action today, covering Jesus's rebuke of his disciples' inability to stay awake all the way through to Judas's betrayal and Jesus's arrest. The scene-ending duet leaves us feeling pure outrage.

Let's start with the narrative recitative. Thus far in the oratorio, the Evangelist recounts the story using a journalistic style. He's impartial and unemotional. Today you'll hear the first crack in the veneer of impassivity that will continue to widen from here on. Jesus also demonstrates a range of emotions that are viewed by Dr. Greenberg as his public and private faces. He's quite stern privately when speaking to the disciples about their inability to keep watch with him but becomes calm when publicly facing Judas.[32]

The duet in No. 27 (*BWV No. 33*) is one of the most compelling reactive pieces of the oratorio. The alto and soprano soloists come from Choir 1 while Choir 2 provides the chorus. Visually in the church this would have communicated a clear dialogue between the dueting women and a group of people represented by the chorus, which begs the question, who are these characters?

Let's back up a bit and start with the instrumental intro. The disciples are witnessing Jesus's betrayal and arrest. The very first emotion depicted by the instruments is utter confusion. The confusion then gives way to rage, and that is what we hear in the chorus: the disciples protesting the arrest. While the sorrowing women duet, the disciples are angry. That anger will eventually transform into fear, but we won't see that until later. Primarily, we hear the dueting women express bewilderment and sorrow at what's unfolding while the disciples weave in and out their impotent protestations.

The women remind me of Susan and Lucy hiding in the bushes watching their beloved Aslan being humiliated, tortured, and killed. There is so much depth of emotion that it feels inconceivable the tension could expand any more, but oh, it does.

In the final chorus both choirs sing together. This happens rarely in the oratorio, so when it does it's worth taking note. In this instance they violently insert themselves as all of Creation, wrathful at the unjust actions they're seeing.[33] Creation, as represented by the two choirs, intertwines its shock, anger, and desire to mete out holy justice on those who would entrap the Lord by echoing their rage back and forth.

Bach uses the music to dramatically mirror Picander's libretto. Thunder, lightning, confusion . . . the music reflects the storm of our own grief at witnessing his arrest and our natural desire to lash out at those we deem responsible. He also gives us a completely different impression of Creation; instead of a passive entity put here for our use it has become something alive with a desire to protect the Creator. We tremble at the horrific idea that Creation can rage and desire humanity's destruction for its grievous crimes against the Son of God.

If you want to harken to the original performance, No. 27 (BWV No. 33) is best heard through surround sound or headphones. The choirs can echo back and forth in your ears giving you a feel for what it would be like to experience the "storm" in person.

The Great Passion

Scripture Reading

Matthew 26:43-50

Listening

Gardiner's recording: Track 26 (2:26); Track 27 (5:28)

Libretto

Track 26 (2:26)
No. 26 Recitative (Evangelist, Jesus, and Judas)
(BWV No. 32)

Evangelist

Und er kam und fand sie aber schlafend, und ihre Augen waren voll Schlafs. Und er ließ sie und ging abermal hin und betete zum drittenmal und redete dieselbigen Worte. Da kam er zu seinen Jüngern und sprach:

Jesus came to the disciples and found them sleeping again because their eyes were so heavy. He left them and went to pray for a third time saying the same thing. Then he came and told his disciples:

Jesus

Ach! wollt ihr nun schlafen und ruhen? Siehe, die Stunde ist hie, dass des Menschen Sohn in der Sünder Hände überantwortet wird. Stehet auf, lasset uns gehen; siehe, er ist da, der mich verrat.

Ah, would you rest now? The hour has come when the Son of Man will be given over to sinners. Get up and let's go. See there, the one who's betraying me has come.

Evangelist

Und als er noch redete, siehe, da kam Judas, der Zwölfen einer, und mit ihm eine große Schar mit Schwertern und mit Stangen von den Hohepriestern und Ältesten des Volks.

While he was talking, Judas came with a great crowd carrying swords and clubs coming from the high priests.

Und der Verräter hatte ihnen
ein Zeichen gegeben und
gesagt: "Welchen ich küssen
werde, der ists, den greifet!"
Und alsbald trat er zu Jesu und
sprach:

Judas had already told them
that the one he kisses is the
man they want. He went up to
Jesus and said:

Judas

Gegrüßet seist du, Rabbi!

Greetings to you, Teacher!

Evangelist

Und küssete ihn. Jesus aber
sprach zu ihm:

As Judas gave him a kiss, Jesus
said:

Jesus

Mein Freund, warum bist du
kommen?

My friend, why do you come?

Evangelist

Da traten sie hinzu und legten
di Hände an Jesum und griffen
ihn.

The crowd came and, putting
their hands on Jesus, arrested
him.

Track 27 (5:28)
No. 27a-27b Duet (Soprano and Alto) and Chorus
(BWV No. 33)

Duet

So ist mein Jesus nun gefan-
gen.

So my Jesus is now arrested.

Chorus

Laßt ihn, haltet, bindet nicht!

Let him go, do not hold or
bind him!

Duet

Mond und Licht	Moon and light
Ist vor Schmerzen untergangen,	Are darkened in sorrow,
Weil mein Jesus ist gefangen.	Because my Jesus is arrested.

Chorus

Laßt ihn, haltet, bindet nicht!	Let him go, do not hold or bind him!

Duet

Sie führen ihn, er ist gebunden.	They take him away, bound.

Chorus

Sind Blitze, sind Donner in Wolken verschwunden?	Has lightning and thunder vanished in the clouds?
Eröffne den feurigen Abgrund, o Hölle,	Hell, open your fiery abyss and
Zertrümmre, verderbe, verschlinge, zerschelle	Crush, destroy, shatter, and devour
Mit plötzlicher Wut	With swift rage
Den falschen Verräter, das mördrische Blut!	The lying friend, the bloodthirsty crowd!

Day 18—Tuesday
(2 minutes)

After the wealth of symbolism and emotion we got yesterday, today is a bit of a breather. The story moves into the end of the first half of the oratorio as we see Jesus arrested and the disciples scattered.

The Great Passion

Scripture Reading

Matthew 26:51-56

Listening

Gardiner's recording: Track 28 (1:48)

Libretto

Track 28 (1:48)
No. 28 Recitative (Evangelist and Jesus)
(BWV No. 34)

Evangelist

Und siehe, einer aus denem, die mit Jesu waren, reckete die Hand aus und schlug des Hohepriesters Knecht und hieb ihm ein Ohr ab. Da sprach Jesus zu ihm:	One of Jesus's group reached out his hand and struck the slave of the high priest, cutting off his ear. Jesus said to him:

Jesus

Stecke dein Schwert an seinen Ort; denn wer das Schwert nimmt, der soll durchs Schwert umkommen.	Put away your sword. All who pick up the sword must die by the sword.

99

Oder meinest du, dass ich nicht könnte meinen Vater bitten, dass er mir zuschickte mehr denn zwölf Legion Engel? Wie würde aber die Schrift erfüllet? Es muss also gehen.

Do you think I cannot ask my Father to send twelve legions of angels? How then would Scripture be fulfilled? It must happen this way.

Evangelist

Zu der Stund sprach Jesus zu den Scharen:

Jesus said to those gathered:

Jesus

Ihr seid ausgegangen als zu einem Mörder, mit Schwerten und mit Stangen, mich zu fahen; bin ich doch täglich bei euch gesessen und habe gelehret im Tempel, und ihr habt mich nicht gegriffen. Aber das ist alles geschehen, dass erfüllet würden die Schriften der Propheten.

You have come against me with swords and clubs as if to arrest a murderer, but I have been with you daily, sitting and teaching in the temple. You have not arrested me at any of those times. All of this has come to pass in this way to fulfill prophesy.

Evangelist

Da verließen ihn alle Jünger und flohen.

Then all the disciples fled and left him alone.

Day 19—Wednesday
(6 minutes)

The proverbial curtain closes on Part One leaving us with the sound of the disciples' feet fleeing into the night as oboes and flutes; listen for them right at the beginning of the chorale.[34] We cannot be reminded too many times of the enormity of Jesus's sacrifice. Bring it up again with your children and acknowledge that our sins, though constantly weighing us down, were borne by him on the cross. Go straight into today's activity with each individual thinking about their own struggles.

The Great Passion

Scripture Reading

No reading

Listening

Gardiner's recording: Track 29 (6:01)

Libretto

Track 29 (6:01)
No. 29 Chorale
(BWV No. 35)

O Mensch, bewein dein Sünde groß,	O man, be sad because of your grievous sin,
Darum Christus seins Vaters Schoß	The Son of God, from his Father's side
Äußert und kam auf Erden;	Came down from heaven;
Von einer Jungfrau rein und zart	Was born of a virgin
Für uns er hie geboren ward,	Was born on earth for us,

Er wollt der Mittler werden.	Willing to stand between us and God.
Den Toten er das Leben gab	He gave life to the dead
Und legt darbei all Krankheit ab,	He healed sickness,
Bis sich die Zeit herdrange,	Until it was time,
Dass er für uns geopfert würd,	For him to be sacrificed for our sins,
Trüg unsrer Sünden schwere Bürd	He carried the weight of our wrongdoing
Wohl an dem Kreuze lange.	To the very cross itself.

Poem

After listening to the chorale, take a moment to read Shakespeare's sonnet (on the facing page) that many scholars consider to be his most overtly Christian in its implications, suggesting that death does not have the final word.[35] In the oratorio we are witnessing all the disciples here, not just Peter, running from their beloved Teacher in his direst and darkest moment. They turn their backs on him and succumb to their basest selves, sulking in unmet expectations of how the Messiah would behave and ultimately bowing to the dominion of fear in their sinful souls: they want to avoid pain and suffering. Shakespeare's sonnet is a rebuke and outpouring of frustration at our constant struggle with sin.

Sonnet 146

William Shakespeare

Poor soul, the center of my sinful earth,
Foiled by these rebel powers that thee array,
Why dost thou pine within and suffer dearth,
Painting thy outward walls so costly gay?
Why so large cost, having so short a lease,
Dost thou upon thy fading mansion spend?
Shall worms, inheritors of this excess,
Eat up thy charge? Is this thy body's end?
Then soul, live thou upon they servant's loss,
And let that pine to aggravate thy store;
Buy terms divine in selling hours of dross;
Within be fed, without be rich no more:
    So shalt thou feed on Death, that feeds on men,
    And, Death once dead, there's no more dying then.

Day 20—Thursday
(5 minutes)

Bach opens the second half of the oratorio with a dialogue between a Daughter of Jerusalem and the Faithful. The alto soloist acting as the Daughter of Jerusalem comes from Choir 1 while the chorus acting as the Faithful responds from Choir 2. Again, by separating the performers physically in the church, the congregation immediately understood that they were witnessing a conversation between those inside the story (Daughter of Jerusalem) and those outside the story (Faithful). Both sides are confused, grieved, and wounded at the fact that their Jesus is really and truly gone. How could this happen? The aria between these two ends on a tension producing chord that leaves the listener feeling as though a question is unanswered, and indeed their question is unanswered until the following number when the Evangelist takes us back to Jesus.[36]

Where is our Savior? He is under trial at the house of the high priest. We have now set the stage for the upward climb to the cross. Peter is in place watching from the shadows as Jesus stands silent before elders and priests who seek out false testimony against him.

The last number is a chorale written from Jesus's perspective. We have no idea what was going on in his head during all of this, but it could be that he was communing with the Father and, even then, seeking protection.

The Great Passion

Scripture Reading

Matthew 26:57-60

Listening

Gardiner's recording: Track 30 (3:30); Track 31 (:53); Track 32 (:39)

Libretto

Track 30 (3:30)
No. 30 Aria (Alto) and Chorus
(BWV No. 36)

Alto

Ach! nun ist mein Jesus hin! Ah! My Jesus has gone.

Chorus

Wo ist denn dein Freund
hingegangen, Where has your friend gone,

O du Schönste unter den
Weibern? O beautiful women?

Alto

Ist es möglich, kann ich
schauen? Is it possible? Can I see it?

Chorus

Wo hat sich dein Freund hing-
ewandt? Where has your friend gone?

Alto

Ach! mein Lamm in Tigerk-
lauen, Ah! My Lamb is in the claws of
a tiger!

Ach! wo ist mein Jesus hin? Ah! Where has my Jesus gone?

Chorus

So wollen wir mit dir ihn
suchen. We will look for him with you.

Alto

Ach! was soll ich der Seele
sagen, What will I tell my soul,

Wenn sie mich wird ängstlich
fragen? When she asks me anxiously?

Ach! wo ist mein Jesus hin? Ah! Where has my Jesus gone?

Track 31 (:53)
No. 31 Recitative (Evangelist)
(BWV No. 37)

Evangelist

Die aber Jesum gegriffen hatten, führeten ihn zu dem Hohepriester Kaiphas, dahin die Schriftgelehrten und Ältesten sich versammlet hatten. Petrus aber folgete ihm nach von ferne bis in den Palast des Hohepriesters und ging hinein und satzte sich bei die Knechte, auf dass er sähe, wo es hinaus wollte. Die Hohepriester aber und Ältesten und der ganze Rat suchten falsche Zeugnis wider Jesum, auf dass sie ihn töteten, und funden keines.

The crowd who seized Jesus took him to the high priest, Caiphas, where the elders and scholars had already gathered. Peter followed them to the palace and sat near the servants to see what would happen. The high priests, elders, scribes, and all gathered there were looking for false witnesses to bring malicious accusations against Jesus so they could execute him. They found no such evidence.

Track 32 (:39)
No. 32 Chorale
(BWV No. 38)

Mir hat die Welt trüglich gericht'
Mit Lügen und mit falschem G'dicht,
Viel Netz und Heimlich Stricke.
Herr, nimm mein wahr in dieser G'fahr,
B'hüt mich für falschen Tücken!

The world has judged me falsely
With lies and malicious gossip,

Secretly woven traps.

Lord, protect me from danger,

Guard me from all malice!

Day 21—Friday
(8½ minutes)

The high priests struggled to find people willing to testify against Jesus, but unfortunately the world is replete with opportunists. Eventually, such individuals were found. The soloists representing the false witnesses are the only soloists who come from Choir 2 in the entire oratorio. Listen closely during their small bit and see if you can hear how Bach has them parroting one another to give them a distinct sheen of deceit. Another bit of storytelling flare comes at the very end of their solo when the instrumentation has a smirky quality to it, just as you would imagine on the face of a bold liar.[37] Jesus is silent during this treatment, a characterization that slides right into the reflective recitative that exudes a deep stillness in the music. Lest we forget how emotional and frustrating all this is, the very next reflective piece is the polar opposite of "stillness" and "silence." The tenor's aria draws us into Jesus's inner thought life bringing a new, albeit extrabiblical, layer of understanding to the story. Jesus isn't placid without intense effort and an inextricable reliance on his heavenly Father. If we are to follow his example in the face of religious persecution, then we, too, must rely on God for our calm response.

Bach consistently uses Jesus's halo to enliven our imaginations. When Jesus does finally speak today, he references heavenly clouds. Pay close attention to the strings accompanying his words and the puffiness they bring to mind in his recitative.

Finally, near the end of today's listening we encounter a *turba* chorus. In the genre of Passion music, and particularly this Passion, a *turba* is any time the chorus is used to represent unruly or mob-like crowds. The classic "crucify him" *turba* is upcoming, but we see a lead up to that pivotal scene in today's narrative when the crowd declares him guilty and worthy of the death sentence.[38] On the back of the *turba*, we watch the guards mock him. Their music is unbalanced mirroring their behavior.

The scene-ending response of the Christian community in the chorale is disbelief at how Jesus is being treated.

There is so much more you could dig into on symbolism within the music as it reflects the action, but giving your children little bits along the way to hook them into listening is all that's necessary to fire their curiosity and keep their attention during a longer listening day like today. This *Passion* is a veritable treasure trove of brilliance, and I encourage you to dig deeper elsewhere to find all the gems. (The books recommended in "Enrichment Resources" are a good start.)

The Great Passion

Scripture Reading

Matthew 26:60-68

Listening

Gardiner's recording: Track 33 (1:02); Track 34 (1:16); Track 35 (3:34); Track 36 (1:55); Track 37 (:42)

Libretto

Track 33 (1:02)
No. 33 Recitative (Evangelist, Witnesses, and High Priest)
(BWV No. 39)

Evangelist

Und wiewohl viel falsche Zeugen herzutraten, funden sie doch keins. Zuletzt traten herzu zween falsche Zeugen und sprachen:	Many false witnesses came to that place, but they didn't bring any evidence against Jesus. Finally, two false witnesses came forward and said:

First and Second Witnesses

Er hat gesagt: Ich kann den
Tempel Gottes abbrechen und
in dreien Tagen denselben
bauen.

He has said, "I can destroy the
Temple of God and rebuild it
in three days."

Evangelist

Und der Hohepriester stund
auf und sprach zu ihm:

The high priest stood up and
said to Jesus:

High Priest

Antwortest du nichts zu dem,
das diese wider dich zeugen?

Do you have nothing to say
about these accusations?

Evangelist

Aber Jesus schwieg stille.

But Jesus stayed silent.

Track 34 (1:16)
No. 34 Recitative (Tenor)
(BWV No. 40)

Mein Jesus schweigt
Zu falschen Lügen stille,
Um uns damit zu zeigen,
Dass sein Erbarmens voller
Wille
Vor uns zum Leiden sei
geneigt,
Und dass wir in dergleichen
Pein
Ihm sollen ähnlich sein
Und in Verfolgung stille sch-
weigen.

My Jesus stays silent
In the face of lies,
In order to show us,
That his mercy's desire

Is set on suffering on our
behalf,
And that we, when in similar
pain
Should copy him
And be silent in times of persecution.

Track 35 (3:34)
No. 35 Aria (Tenor)
(BWV No. 41)

Geduld!
Wenn mich falsche Zungen
stechen.
Lei dich wider meine Schuld

Schimpf und Spott,
Ei, so mag der liebe Gott
Meines Herzens Unschuld
rachen.

Patience!
Even though liars come at me.

Even though I suffer and am
innocent
They make fun,
So may the loving God
Give vengeance to my inno-
cent heart.

Track 36 (1:55)
No. 36a-36d Recitative (Evangelist, High Priest, Jesus, and Chorus)
(BWV Nos. 42-43)

Evangelist
Und der Hohepriester antwortete und sprach zu ihm:

The high priest answered him
and said:

High Priest
Ich beschwöre dich be idem
lebendigen Gott, dass du uns
sagest, ob du seiest Christus,
der Sohn Gottes?

In the name of God, I command you to say whether or
not you are the Christ, the Son
of God?

Evangelist
Jesus sprach zu ihm:

Jesus answered:

Jesus
Du sagest's. Doch sage ich
euch:

So you say. But I say to you:

Von nun an wird's gesche-
hen, dass ihr sehen werdet
des Menschen Sohn sitzen
zur Rechten der Kraft und
kommen in den Wolken des
Himmels.

From now on you will see the
Son of Man sitting at God's
right hand and coming on
heavenly clouds.

Evangelist

Da zerriss der Hohepriester
seine Kleider und sprach:

On hearing this, the high
priest tore his clothes and
said:

High Priest

Er hat Gott gelästert; was
dürfen wir weiter Zeugnis?
Siehe, itzt habt ihr seine
Gotteslästerung gehöret. Was
dünket euch?

You've blasphemed against
God! What need is there for
more witnesses? Right here
all of you have heard him
blaspheme God. What's your
verdict?

Evangelist

Sie antworteten und sprachen:

They answered:

Chorus

Er ist des Todes schuldig!

He is guilty and should be put
to death!

Evangelist

Da speieten sie aus in sein
Angesicht und schlugen ihn
mit Fäusten. Etliche aber
schlugen ihn ins Angesicht
und sprachen:

They spat on his face and
punched him. While hitting
his face some of them said:

Chorus

Weissage uns, Christe, wer
ist's, der dich schlug?

Prophesy to us, Christ! Who's
hitting you?

Track 37 (:42)
No. 37 Chorale
(BWV No. 44)

Wer hat dich so geschlagen,	Who has knocked you about,
Mein Heil, und dich mit Plagen	My Savior, and with menace
So übel zugericht'?	Battered you so horribly?
Du bist ja nicht ein Sünder	You aren't a sinner
Wie wir und unsre Kinder;	Like the rest of us;
Von Missetaten weist.	Of sins you know nothing.

Day 22—Saturday

Activities

Reading

The Warden and the Wolf King by Andrew Peterson, chapter 94, "The Seed is Planted"

Listening

The Gray Havens's song "This is My Soul" from the album *Ghost of a King*

Open your time together by listening to the song "This My Soul" from The Gray Havens. Read aloud chapter 94 "The Seed is Planted" from *The Warden and the Wolf King* by Andrew Peterson. This is the fourth and final book in *The Wingfeather Saga*, and chapter 94 is a spoiler. Read at your own risk if you haven't read the series! Peterson did not make the story overtly Christian, but deep truths shine through, nonetheless. The themes of facing our own worst natures and sacrificing self to something greater are foundational to these stories and culminate in this charged chapter. These themes are also integral to Lent.

Sunday

Read the following poem from *The Songs of Innocence and Experience* by William Blake. The art of ministering well to each other in times of grief can feel scary and intimidating. Will we say/do/be the right thing for those in pain? Blake cuts the knees out from under this anxiety by reminding us that sorrowing alongside others without trying to fix them or their problems is a way God reaches through us to us. It is him in us sitting quietly like Job's friends before they opened their mouths. Pray for God's grace to flow through you to those in mourning around you, and for the courage and grace to sit with them while their tumultuous waves of sorrow swirl.

Poem

On Another's Sorrow
WILLIAM BLAKE

Can I see another's woe,
And not be in sorrow too?
Can I see another's grief,
And not seek for kind relief?

Can I see a falling tear,
And not feel my sorrow's share?
Can a father see his child
Weep, nor be with sorrow filled?

Can a mother sit and hear
An infant groan, an infant fear?
No, no! never can it be!
Never, never can it be!

And can He who smiles on all
Hear the wren with sorrows small,
Hear the small bird's grief and care,
Hear the woes that infants bear—

And not sit beside the next,
Pouring pity in their breast,
And not sit the cradle near,
Weeping tear on infant's tear?

And not sit both night and day,
Wiping all our tears away?
Oh no! never can it be!
Never, never can it be!

He doth give his joy to all:
He becomes an infant small,
He becomes a man of woe,
He doth feel the sorrow too.

Think not thou canst sigh a sigh,
And thy Maker is not by:
Think not thou canst weep a tear,
And thy Maker is not near.

Oh He gives to us his joy,
That our grief he may destroy:
Till our grief is fled and gone
He doth sit by us and moan.

Week Five

Wherefore I all forgo:
To one word only I say, No:
Where in the deed there was an intimation
Of a gift or donation,
Lord, let it now by way of purchase go.

—GEORGE HERBERT IN "OBEDIENCE"

Day 23—Monday
(9 minutes)

Peter's three denials of Jesus are upon us, and today we will sit with him in his grief. He had hoped for a better response from himself, but when it came down to the choice between faith and fear, he chose fear. Listen to the music, read the poem, and let it lie. Don't over-lecture or preach on this one; allow the art to speak for itself.

Look out for the violin interlacing the soloist's aria "Erbarme dich." This number represents Peter's inner voice, but it is also applicable to all of Christendom, and it absolutely weeps.[39]

The Great Passion

Scripture Reading

Matthew 26:69-75

Listening

Gardiner's recording: Track 38 (2:18); Track 39 (6:43)

Libretto

Track 38 (2:18)
Nos. 38a-38c Recitative (Evangelist, First and Second Maids, Peter, and Chorus)
(BWV Nos. 45-46)

Evangelist

Petrus aber saß draußen im Palast; und es trat zu ihm eine Magd und sprach:	While Peter sat outside a maid came to him and said:

First Maid

Und du warest auch mit dem
Jesu aus Galiläa.

You were with Jesus of Galilee.

Evangelist

Er leugnete aber vor ihnen
allen und sprach:

He denied it before everyone
standing there and said:

Peter

Ich weiß nicht, was du sagest.

I don't know what you're
talking about.

Evangelist

Als er aber zur Tür hinaus-
ging, sahe ihn eine andere und
sprach zu denen, die da waren:

When he left, another maid
saw him and said to those
nearby:

Second Maid

Dieser war auch mit dem Jesu
von Nazareth.

That man was with Jesus of
Nazareth.

Evangelist

Und er leugnete abermal und
schwur dazu:

He swore and denied it again
saying:

Peter

Ich kenne des Menschen nicht.

I don't know the man.

Evangelist

Und über eine kleine Weile
traten hinzu, die da stunden,
und sprachen zu Petro:

After a little longer, those
standing near Peter came to
him and said:

Chorus

Wahrlich, du bist auch
einer von denen; denn deine
Sprache verrät dich.

Seriously, you must have been
one of his followers! The way
you talk tells us you were one
of them.

Evangelist

Da hub er an, sich zu ver-
fluchen und zu schwören:

Peter began swearing in frustration and said again:

Peter

Ich kenne des Menschen nicht.

I don't know the man.

Evangelist

Und alsbald krähete der Hahn.
Da dachte Petrus an die Worte
Jesu, da er zu ihm sagte: Ehe
der Hahn krähen wird, wirst
du mich dreimal verleugnen.
Und ging heraus und weinete
bitterlich.

Right then the rooster crowed.
Peter remembered Jesus
telling him that he would deny
Jesus three times before that
crow. When he realized all
that had come to pass, Peter
left and cried bitterly.

Track 39 (6:43)
No. 39 Aria (Alto)
(BWV No. 47)

Erbarme dich,
Mein Gott, um meiner Zähren
willen!
Schaue hier,
Herz und Auge weint vor dir
Bitterlich.

Have mercy,
My God, for the sake of my
tears!
Look at me,
My heart and eyes cry to you
Bitterly.

Dive straight into the reading of this poem without belaboring meaning. Again, just let the art of Bach's and Chatterton's work speak for itself.

The Resignation

THOMAS CHATTERTON

O God, whose thunder shakes the sky,
Whose eye this atom globe surveys,
To thee, my only rock, I fly,
Thy mercy in thy justice praise.

The mystic mazes of thy will,
The shadows of celestial light,
Are past the power of human skill,
But what the Eternal acts is right.

O teach me in the trying hour,
When anguish swells the dewy tear,
To still my sorrows, own thy power,
Thy goodness love, thy justice fear.

If in this bosom aught but Thee,
Encroaching sought a boundless sway,
Omniscience could the danger see,
And Mercy look the cause away.

Then why, my soul, dost thou complain?
Why drooping seek the dark recess?
Shake off the melancholy chain,
For God created all to bless.

But ah! My breast is human still;
The rising sigh, the falling tear,
My languid vitals' feeble rill,
The sickness of my soul declare.

But yet, with fortitude resigned,
I'll thank the inflictor of the blow;
Forbid the sigh, compose my mind,
Nor let the gush of misery flow.

The gloomy mantle of the night,
Which on my sinking spirit steals,
Will vanish at the morning light,
Which God, my East, my sun reveals.

Day 24—Tuesday
(8½ minutes)

The selection of songs today comes from Scenes 5 and 6 covering Judas's remorse and Jesus before Pilate, so we're bouncing between two different settings.

The first scene is focused on Judas and the priests. Oh, tragic Judas. Straight off the bat we enter his guilt-ridden head through the chorale in which he laments the part he has played in the unfolding drama. I don't think it's an accident that this chorale mirrors what is going on inside of Peter whom we just left weeping bitterly. Peter and Judas are cohabitating an identity as disciples who betrayed or rejected Jesus. Both are at a crossroads in their guilt and shame. One chooses to humble himself before his Lord, the other chooses grasping attempts to fix the mistake while not repenting fully. It is Cain and Abel playing out all over again, and the consequences are familiar. The chorale sits at this crossroads and can be attributed to either character. That being said, it is linked to Judas's remorse, not the previous scene where we left Peter sorrowing over his mistake. I believe we're intentionally being shown Judas's unity with Peter in this moment. The dichotomy between the chorale and Judas's outward response also demonstrates that we can know and say the right things, but ultimately not allow them to permeate into our being. Judas knows these words; he's been one of Jesus's intimates for years! But his story takes a turn, and the actions he chooses in response to his mistake ultimately lead away from humility and forgiveness into destruction. Instead of seeking forgiveness from God, he tries to return the money and absolve himself in his own power. When the priests don't allow him that liberty, he kills himself.

We then shift settings to the palace. Jesus is standing before Pilate, a man overwhelmed at his position between a person he knows to be innocent, that person's false accusers, and political expectations that demand certain actions of him. Pilate is conflicted and will remain so for the duration of the narrative.

There are a few things to be looking out for as you listen today. When the priests declare the money to be unclean, they sound piously disgusted. The phenomenal ability of Bach to bring to life a personality type through instrumentation and voice continually astounds me. This is a standout moment in this respect; they just sound so exactly like they're sticking their noses up! Also, listen carefully to the last bit of the Evangelist's narrative as he highlights Jesus's silent response by going higher on *Wort* which can be translated as "word" or "speech" or "response." Finally, today is the third instance of "O Sacred Head, Now Wounded." It leaves us with the scene-ending expression of comfort and adoration.[40]

My eldest daughter commented that she felt sure Bach intentionally brought to life Judas's hanging through the instrumentation. I, honestly, did not notice nor have I found anything in the scholarship pointing this out. However, I think it's ever so important to let your kids begin to interpret the oratorio and take ownership of what they're hearing. Did I respond to her by saying, "Well, you know, in fact there is no scholarship backing up your claim." No, certainly not. Let your kids hear the story with their own ears without fear that they're "getting it wrong." They're not!

The Great Passion

Scripture Reading

Matthew 27:1-14

Listening

Gardiner's recording: Track 40 (:54), Track 41 (1:43), Track 42 (2:53), Track 43 (2:01), Track 44 (:58)

Libretto

Track 40 (:54)
No. 40 Chorale
(BWV No. 48)

Bin ich gleich von dir gewichen,	Even though I left your side,
Stell ich mich doch wieder ein;	I returned;
Hat uns doch dein Sohn verglichen	Because your Son has restored me to you
Durch sein' Angst und Todespein.	Through his suffering and death.
Ich verleugne nicht die Schuld;	I do not deny my sin;
Aber deine Gnad und Huld	But your grace and mercy
Ist viel größer als die Sünde,	Far exceed my sins,
Die ich stets in mir befinde.	That I'm constantly aware of.

Track 41 (1:43)
Nos. 41a-41c Recitative (Evangelist, Judas, Chorus, First and Second High Priests)
(BWV Nos. 49-50)

Evangelist

Des Morgens aber hielten alle Hohepriester und die Ältesten des Volks einen Rat über Jesum, dass sie ihn töteten. Und bunden ihn, führeten ihn hin und überantworteten ihn dem Landpfleger Pontio Pilato. Da das sahe Judas, der ihn verraten hatte, dass er verdammt war zum Tode, gereuete es ihn und brachte herwieder die dreißig Silberlinge den Hohepriestern und Ältesten und sprach:

In the morning, all those gathered against Jesus discussed how they could succeed in putting him to death. Tying him up, they handed him over to the governor, Pontius Pilate. When Judas the Betrayer saw that Jesus would be condemned to die, he regretted what he had done. He took back the thirty pieces of silver to the high priests saying:

Judas

Ich habe übel getan, dass ich unschuldig Blut verraten habe.

I have sinned by betraying an innocent man.

Evangelist

Sie sprachen:

They said:

Chorus

Was gehet uns das an?
Da siehe du zu!

What have we to do with that?
Figure that out yourself.

Evangelist

Und er warf die Silberlinge in
den Tempel, hub sich davon,
ging hin und erhängete sich
selbst. Aber die Hohepriester
nahmen die Silberlinge und
sprachen:

Judas threw the pieces of silver
into the temple, immediately
left that place, and hanged
himself. The high priests
picked up the money and said:

First and Second High Priest

Es taugt nicht, dass wir sie in
den Gotteskasten legen, denn
es ist Blutgeld.

This is blood money so we
can't lawfully put it into the
temple treasury.

Track 42 (2:53)
No. 42 Aria (Bass)
(BWV No. 51)

Gebt mir meinen Jesum wieder!
Seht, das Geld, den Mörder-
lohn,
Wirft euch der verlorne Sohn

Zu den Füßen nieder!

Give me back my Jesus!

See, the blood money given to
pay for his murderer's reward,
The wayward son throws at
you
Down at your feet!

Track 43 (2:01)
No. 43 Recitative (Evangelist, Pilate, and Jesus)
(BWV No. 52)

Evangelist

Sie hielten aber einen Rat und kauften einen Töpfersacker darum zum Begräbnis der Pilger. Daher ist derselbige Acker genennet der Blutacker bis auf den heutigen Tag. Da ist erfüllet, das gesagt ist durch den Propheten Jeremias, da er spricht: "Sie haben genommen dreißig Silberlinge, damit bezahlet ward der Verkaufte, welchen sie kauften von den Kindern Israel, und haben sie gegeben um einen Töpfersacker, als mir der Herr befohlen hat." Jesus aber stund vor dem Landpfleger; und der Landpfleger fragte ihn und sprach:

The high priests talked together again to try and decide what to do with the thirty pieces of silver. In the end, they decided to buy a potter's field that was designated as a burial site. That field is known as the "Field of Blood" to this day, fulfilling a prophecy made by Jeremiah where he said, "They took the thirty pieces of silver used to buy the man from the children of Israel, and they bought a potter's field, as the Lord commanded me." But Jesus stood before the governor who questioned him and said:

Pilate

Bist du der Jüden König?

Are you the King of the Jews?

Evangelist

Jesus aber sprach zu ihm:

Jesus answered him:

Jesus

Du sagest's.

You say so.

Evangelist

Und da er verklagt war von den Hohepriestern und Ältesten, antwortete er nichts. Da sprach Pilatus zu ihm:

When the high priests made their charge against him, Jesus said nothing. Pilate said to him:

Pilate

Hörest du nicht, wie hart sie
dich verklagen?

Do you not hear how aggressively they accuse you?

Evangelist

Und er antwortete ihm nicht
auf ein Wort, also, dass sich
auch der Landpfleger sehr
verwunderte.

Jesus never gave a response,
which bewildered the
governor.

Track 44 (:58)
No. 44 Chorale
(BWV No. 53)

Befiehl du deine Wege
Und was dein Herze kränkt
Der allertreusten Pflege

Entrust your ways
And what grieves your heart
To the utmost faithful care of
him

Des, der den Himmel lenkt.
Der Wolken, Luft und Winden

Who governs heaven.
He, who gives clouds, air, and
winds

Gibt Wege, Lauf und Bahn,
Der wird auch Wege finden,
Da dein Fuß gehen kann.

Their paths, course, and track,
He will also find the path,
Where your feet can tread.

Day 25—Wednesday
(3 minutes)

The two prominent *turbae* of the oratorio occur today when the people demand Pilate release Barabbas over Jesus and cry out their desire to crucify him. Listen for an extreme jump in emotional expression from the discordant and chaotic rage of the crowd to the grief of the chorale.[41] Bach uses this musical contrast to highlight the bloodthirsty nature of the people by following up the *turbae* with a strong, still melody, reminding us that it is our own tendency towards animalistic violence that requires this sacrifice of Jesus.

The Great Passion

Scripture Reading

Matthew 27:15-22

Listening

Gardiner's recording: Track 45 (2:09), Track 46 (:38)

Libretto

Track 45 (2:09)
Nos. 45a-45b Recitative (Evangelist, Pilate, Pilate's Wife, and Chorus)
(BWV No. 54)

Evangelist

Auf das Fest aber hatte der Landpfleger Gewohnheit, dem Volk einen Gefangenen los-zugeben, welchen sie wollten.

Every Passover the governor traditionally set free a prisoner chosen by the people.

Er hatte aber zu der Zeit einen Gefangenen, einen sonderlichen vor andern, der hieß Barrabas. Und da sie versammlet waren, sprach Pilatus zu ihnen:

At that time, he had an infamous prisoner named Barabbas, and when they had all gathered he said to them:

Pilate

Welchen wollet ihr, dass ich euch losgebe? Barrabam oder Jesum, von dem gesaget wird, er sei Christus?

Which man do you want me to set free? Barabbas or Jesus, whom some say is the Christ?

Evangelist

Denn er wusste wohl, dass sie ihn aus Neid überantwortet hatten. Und da er auf dem Richtstuhl saß, schickete sein Weib zu ihm und ließ ihm sagen:

Pilate knew the leaders had brought Jesus to him out of jealousy. His wife sent for him and said:

Pilate's Wife

Habe du nichts zu schaffen mit diesem Gerechten; ich habe heute viel erlitten im Traum von seinetwegen!

Don't have anything to do with this righteous man; I have suffered greatly in a dream because of him!

Evangelist

Aber die Hohenpriester und die Ältesten überredeten das Volk, dass sie um Barrabam bitten sollten und Jesum umbrächten. Da antwortete nun der Landpfleger und sprach zu ihnen:

The high priests and elders had gone throughout the crowd persuading the people to ask for Barabbas and to demand that Jesus be killed. The governor said to them:

Pilate

Welchen wollt ihr unter diesen zweien, den ich euch soll losgeben?

Which of these two men do I set free?

Evangelist

Sie sprachen:

They said:

Chorus

Barrabum!

Barabbas!

Evangelist

Pilatus sprach zu ihnen:

Pilate said to them:

Pilate

Was soll lich denn machen mit Jesu, von dem gesagt wird, er sei Christus?

What should I do with Jesus whom some say is the Christ?

Evangelist

Sie sprachen alle:

They all said:

Chorus

Laß ihn kreuzigen!

Crucify him!

Track 46 (:38)
No. 46 Chorale
(BWV No. 55)

Wie wunderbarlich ist doch diese Strafe!
Der gute Hirte leidet für die Schafe,
Die Schuld bezahlt der Herre, der Gerechte,
Für seine Knechte.

How marvelous is this punishment!
The good Shepherd suffers for the sheep,
The righteous master pays the price,
For his servants.

Day 26—Thursday
(6½ minutes)

The soloist in the recitative is answering Pilate's question about Jesus's guilt by declaring his good works rather than attacking the accusers. The aria then asserts that Jesus is being falsely accused, but in love he is choosing to die as the innocent sacrifice. It must be this way.

The Great Passion

Scripture Reading

Matthew 27:23

Listening

Gardiner's recording: Track 47 (:14), Track 48 (1:05), Track 49 (5:19)

Libretto

Track 47 (:14)
No. 47 Recitative (**Evangelist and Pilate**)
(BWV No. 56)

Evangelist

Der Landpfleger sagte: The governor then said:

Pilate

Was hat er denn Übels getan?   What evil has he done?

Track 48 (1:05)
No. 48 Recitative (**Soprano**)
(BWV No. 57)

Er hat uns allen wohlgetan,
Den Blinden gab er das Gesicht,
Die Lahmen macht er gehend,
Er sagt uns seines Vaters Wort,
Er trieb die Teufel fort,
Betrübte hat er aufgericht',
Er nahm die Sünder auf und an.
Sonst hat mein Jesus nichts getan.

He has done good to all of us,
He gave sight to the blind,
He made the lame walk,
He taught us his Father's word,
He drove away demons,
The distressed he raised up,
He welcomed and embraced sinners.
My Jesus has done nothing else.

Track 49 (5:19)
No. 49 Aria (Soprano)
(BWV No. 58)

Aus Liebe will mein Heiland sterben,
Von einer Sünde weiß er nichts.

Out of love my Savior is willing to die,
He doesn't know anything of sin.

Dass das ewige Verderben
Und die Strafe des Gerichts

So that eternal ruin
And the punishment of judgement

Nicht auf meiner Seele bliebe.

My soul won't have to bear.

133

Day 27—Friday
(9½ minutes)

Bach intensifies the second "crucify him" *turba* by making it short, sharp, and leaving it unfinished in our ears.[42] The people want blood, and blood Pilate will give though trying to clean his hands of it. When the people accept the responsibility for his death, it is with a final *turba*. For centuries this portion of the Gospel of Matthew, where the Jews accept responsibility for his blood, has been used aggressively against them to justify anti-Semitic behavior. Some people see Bach's Passions as problematic because of this question of blame. If you truly absorb this work in its entirety, the message Bach is communicating is that, yes, here is what happened on that fateful day. But the "what happened" doesn't answer the "why did it happen" and those are very different questions. The blame clearly rests on all of humanity, and we have spent, and will continue to spend, a considerable amount of time contemplating our part in all of this. The crowd represented in this *turba* is us, the listeners, and it ends forcefully in D major giving our ears a satisfying finality. Bach uses this technique to communicate to us that Jesus's fate is now sealed.[43] Through Picander's poetry we know that it is sealed by our own sins, not the Jews alone. Let's step into one of those reflections now.

The soloist beseeches God to witness the injustices happening to Jesus by using E minor, the key symbolizing crucifixion for Bach.[44] There is anger represented both in the voice and in the dotted strings. The singer shifts her focus away from God and onto the tormenters by begging them to stop their abuse, but we know it's to no avail because we are those tormentors. The dotted strings carry through into the aria but are slowed way down. The soloist ends the scene by expressing our deep longing amidst our utter powerlessness to help ease Jesus's suffering. So much grief. So much faith.

The Great Passion

Scripture Reading

Matthew 27:24-26

Listening

Gardiner's recording: Track 50 (1:50), Track 51 (:57), Track 52 (6:49)

Libretto

Track 50 (1:50)
No. 50a-50e Recitative (Evangelist, Chorus, and Pilate)
(BWV No. 59)

Evangelist

Sie schrieen aber noch mehr und sprachen:	They cried again louder and said:

Chorus

Laß ihn kreuzigen!	Crucify him!

Evangelist

Da aber Pilatus sahe, dass er nichts schaffete, sondern dass ein viel großer Getummel ward, nahm er Wasser und wusch die Hände vor dem Volk und sprach:	When Pilate saw that he couldn't convince the crowd as they grew more hostile, he washed his hands with water in front of the people and said:

Pilate

Ich bin unschuldig an dem Blut dieses Gerechten, sehet ihr zu.	I'm not guilty of this innocent man's blood. It is up to you.

Evangelist

Da antwortete das ganze Volk und sprach:	After seeing this, the people cried:

Chorus

Sein Blut komme über uns und unsre Kinder.	Let the guilt of his blood be on us and our children.

Evangelist

Da gab er ihnen Barrabam los; aber Jesum ließ er geißeln und überantwortete ihn, dass er gekreuziget würde.	He set Barabbas free to the crowd, but had Jesus whipped and sent him to be crucified.

Track 51 (:57)
No. 51 Recitative (Alto)
(BWV No. 60)

Erbarm es Gott!	Have mercy, God!
Hier steht der Heiland angebunden.	Here the Savior stands bound.
O Geißelung, o Schläg, o Wunden!	O scourging, o blows, o wounds!
Ihr Henker, haltet ein!	You hangmen, stop!
Erweichet euch	Does not
Der Seelen Schmerz,	The sight of such pain,
Der Anblick solches Jammers nicht?	Soften your hearts?
Ach ja! ihr habt ein Herz,	Ah yes! You have a heart,
Das muss der Martersäule gleich	That must be like a whipping post
Und noch viel härter sein.	Or harder still.
Erbarmt euch, haltet ein!	Have mercy, stop!

Track 52 (6:49)
No. 52 Aria (Alto)
(BWV No. 61)

Können Tränen meiner Wan-
gen
Nichts erlangen,
O, so nehmt mein Herz hinein!
Aber laßt es bei den Fluten,
Wenn die Wunden milde
bluten,
Auch die Opferschale sein!

If the tears on my cheeks can

Accomplish nothing,
Oh, then take my heart!
It, in the midst of the streaming,
Bleeding wounds,

To be the sacrificial cup!

Day 28—Saturday

Activities

Reading
Tales of the Resistance by David and Karen Mains, pages 105-107

Listening
Nickel Creek's song "Doubting Thomas" from the album *Why Should the Fire Die?*

Pull back out the book *Tales of the Resistance* by David and Karen Mains from *Kingdom Tales Trilogy*. Stick to the italicized portion from pages 105-107, and the story will pick up where we left off.

I was first introduced to these books as a child. My mom borrowed them from a friend for a short time leaving my sister and I totally entranced. The writing is imaginative and lovely, but the illustrations really imprinted themselves on our minds. When those books left our house to return to their original owner, we moved on to other things. Years later as young adults, my sister and I had a serious conversation about whether those stories we barely remembered, but also could not forget, were books or movies. The images hung onto the edges of our memories so intensely and with such vibrancy that we honestly didn't know whether we read them or watched them. My mom had zero recollection of it, and neither of us could come up with a name. We mourned the loss, sure we would never locate the original material since we couldn't even be sure of its medium! When I first lived in Papua New Guinea, I stayed with a couple who had been on the field for decades and were good friends with my parents. Imagine my surprise when I saw those books on their shelves in the middle of the PNG Highlands, and all of it came flooding back. She was the one who lent them to my mother all those years ago during a short home assignment! The words and pictures had rooted themselves firmly in my imagination bringing to life later understanding of God's character in ways that simply wouldn't have come to pass without the tilling work of that story well told and beautifully illustrated.

The characters in *Narnia*, *Wingfeather*, and the *Kingdom Tales* all have one thing in common: they all doubt at some point. They hit the darkest parts of their stories when unsettling questions invade their thoughts and sometimes their actions. Even if you don't have access to the *Kingdom Tales Trilogy*, spend time today talking to your kids about doubt, and its ever-present role in our faith life. It happens, and we can't shirk from it or pretend it away. Looking to music, works of art, stories, and, most importantly, the Bible itself, we find fellow doubters on the road. The doubting isn't the problem, it's what we do with it.

Finish today listening to "Doubting Thomas" from Nickel Creek. It's a go-to song for me when I'm wandering and stumbling in the dark. This song is wandering and stumbling, but it lands where we always should:

Doubting Thomas (Excerpt)
NICKEL CREEK

> Please forgive me for the time that I've wasted
> I'm a doubting Thomas
> I'll take your promise
> Though I know nothing's safe
> Oh me of little faith

Sunday

Start your time together by reading this Robert Herrick poem and follow it up by listening to "Behold," a single from Sara Groves featuring Propaganda, Audrey Assad, and Ellie Holcomb (included in the Spotify playlist, see page 202). This song is a collision of different cultures that, both in word and feel, announce unity within the church under what Christ did for all of us, no matter our race or culture or musical preference. As we make our way through one of the most powerful pieces of music composed by a European, it's important to stretch our musical muscles in many directions.

Poem

His Savior's Words, Going to the Cross
ROBERT HERRICK

Have, have ye no regard, all ye
Who pass this way, to pity me,
Who am a man of misery!

A man both bruised and broke, and one
Who suffers not here for mine own,
But for my friends' transgression!

Ah! Sion's Daughters, do not fear
The cross, the cords, the nails, the spear,
The myrrh, the gall, the vinegar:

For Christ, your loving Savior, hath
Drunk up the wine of God's fierce wrath;
Only, there's left a little froth,

Less for to taste, than for to show,
What bitter cups had been your due,
Had He not drunk them up for you.

Week Six

He that will pass his land,
As I have mine, may set his hand
And heart unto this deed, when he hath read;
And make the purchase spread
To both our goods, if he to it will stand.

—GEORGE HERBERT IN "OBEDIENCE"

Day 29—Monday
(3 minutes)

It has happened; the scourge is complete, and the thorns are on Jesus's brow. The compelling "O Sacred Head, Now Wounded" melody, originally written in the 1500s as a bawdy love song, now pulses with the sacred. Bach highlights this fourth of the five instances it's used by making it twice as long as the others. He also sheds the Evangelist's impartial observer role. From here on, the Evangelist will narrate with emotionally charged recitatives carrying us through the darkest parts of the story by reflecting back what we feel each time we wrestle with the deep injustice and endlessly shocking mercy of Jesus's sacrifice.[45]

The Great Passion

Scripture Reading

Matthew 27:27-30

Listening

Gardiner's recording: Track 53 (1:00), Track 54 (1:47)

Libretto

Track 53 (1:00)
No. 53a-53c Recitative (Evangelist and Chorus)
(BWV No. 62)

Evangelist

Da nahmen die Kriegsknechte des Landpflegers Jesum zu sich in das Richthaus	After this, the governor's soldiers took Jesus into the praetorium,

und sammleten über ihn die ganze Schar und zogen ihn aus und legten ihm einen Purpurmantel an und flochten eine dorne Krone und satzten sie auf sein Haupt und ein Rohr in seine rechte Hand und beugeten die Knie vor ihm und spotteten ihn und sprachen:	and after they were all there they stripped him, put on a purple robe, and crowned him with the crown of thorns. They put a reed in his right hand and began to kneel in front of him, mocking him. They said:

Chorus

Gegrüßet seist du, Jüdenkönig!	Hail, King of the Jews!

Evangelist

Und speieten ihn an und nahmen das Rohr und schlugen damit sein Haupt.	They spat on him, and taking back the reed, they beat him in the head with it.

Track 54 (1:47)
No. 54 Chorale
(BWV No. 63)

O Haupt, voll Blut und Wunden,	O head, full of blood and wounds,
Voll Schmerz und voller Hohn,	Full of sorrow and ridicule,
O Haupt, zu Spott gebunden	O head, crowned in mocking cruelty
Mit einer Dornenkron,	With a circle of thorns,
O Haupt, sonst schön gezieret	O head, beautifully decorated before
Mit höchster Ehr und Zier,	With highest respect and honor,
Jetz aber hoch schimpfieret,	But now scorned,
Gegrüßet seist du mir!	I welcome you!
Du edles Angesichte,	Your noble face,
Dafür sonst schrickt und scheut	That bears the terror and dread

143

Das große Weltgerichte,
Wie bist du so bespeit;
Wie bist du so erbleichet!
Wer hat dein Augenlicht,

Dem sonst kein Licht nicht
gleichet,
So schändlich zugericht'?

Of Judgement Day,
How you are spit upon;
How pale you are!
Who has battered the light in
your eyes,
Light without equal,

So shamefully?

Day 30—Tuesday
(7½ minutes)

W e're carrying on in the story with more humiliation. The soldiers mock Jesus mercilessly and march him to Golgotha, but there is a point at which Jesus cannot physically bear the cross any longer. Simon of Cyrene is commanded to carry the cross for him, wherein the soloists respond with a desire to actively participate in taking the load from our Lord. Listen for the depth of instrumentation accompanying the soloist in the aria bringing to the number a heaviness embodying the idea of carrying burdens.[46]

Scripture Reading

Matthew 27:31-32

Listening

Gardiner's recording: Track 55 (:53), Track 56 (:32), Track 57 (6:07)

Libretto

Track 55 (:53)
No. 55 Recitative (Evangelist)
(BWV No. 64)

Evangelist

Und da sie ihn verspottet hatten, zogen sie ihm den Mantel aus und zogen ihm seine Kleider an und führeten ihn hin, dass sie ihn kreuzigten.	After the soldiers mocked him, they took off the purple robe, put on his own clothes, and took him away to crucify him.

145

Und indem sie hinausgingen, funden sie einen Menschen von Kyrene mit Namen Simon; den zwungen sie, dass er ihm sein Kreuz trug.	As they went they met a man from Cyrene named Simon and forced him to carry the cross.

Track 56 (:32)
No. 56 Recitative (Bass)
(BWV No. 65)

Ja freilich will in uns das Fleisch und Blut Zum Kreuz gezwungen sein; Je mehr es unsrer Seele gut,	Certainly, the flesh and blood Forced onto the cross; The more goodness it brings to our souls,
Je herber geht es ein.	The heavier it is to bear.

Track 57 (6:07)
No. 57 Aria (Bass)
(BWV No. 66)

Komm, süßes Kreuz, so will ich sagen, Mein Jesu, gib es immer her! Wird mir mein Leiden einst zu schwer,	Come, sweet cross, I will then say, My Jesus, give it to me. If my pain becomes too much,
So hilfst du mir es selber tragen.	Help me carry it.

Day 31—Wednesday
(5 minutes)

While Jesus suffers on the cross, the people come and go, alternately mocking him and trying to alleviate his pain. It's good to remember that not all the people surrounding him at this point were belligerent non-believers. There were many witnesses who loved him and endured watching the horror of all that was unfolding.

Bach pauses the story after the narrative recitative to allow the soloist a lamentation of the world's rejection of Jesus. In the narrative, we absorb two more *turbae* from the chorus. The second *turba*, when the chief priests and elders get involved, is one in which to sit up and take note. The choirs are used for antiphony. The sounds collide in riotous harmony as the two sides go back and forth mocking Jesus's kingship. Rarely in these antiphonic moments does Bach draw the two choirs together for a unified declaration, but he does so here and because he does it here, it's worth a pondering.[47] They all sing the last bit together, mocking him with his claim to be the Son of God. Is this a point of dramatic irony where the congregants knew, as we do now, that the claim is in fact true while those mocking him in the narrative do not? Or is Bach using their own speech against them? They weaponized the claim against Jesus, but Bach draws them into one united declaration of truth despite themselves. We may never know what he intended by vocally highlighting that line right at that point, but it's something to ponder together.

Bach did slow the story to reflect on the world's rejection of Jesus, so use this pause as an opportunity to stop and discuss how you might be rejecting Jesus in your own heart and life.

The Great Passion

Scripture Reading

Matthew 27:33-44

Listening

Gardiner's recording: Track 58 (3:26), Track 59 (1:25)

Libretto

Track 58 (3:26)
No. 58a-58e Recitative (Evangelist and Chorus)
(BWV Nos. 67-68)

Evangelist

Un da sie an die Stätte kamen mit Namen Golgatha, das ist verdeutschet Schädelstätt, gaben sie ihm Essig zu trinken mit Gallen vermischet; und da er's schmeckete, wollte er's nicht trinken. Da sie ihn aber gekreuziget hatten, teilten sie seine Kleider und wurfen das Los darum, auf dass erfüllet würde, das gesagt ist durch den Propheten:

When they came to Golgotha, called the Place of the Skull, they gave him vinegar mixed with gall to drink. When he tasted some, he refused to drink. After they crucified him, they divided up his clothes by casting lots fulfilling what the prophets said:

"Sie haben meine Kleider unter sich geteilet, und über mein Gewand haben sie das Los geworfen."

"They have divided up all my clothes among themselves by casting lots."

148

Und sie saßen allda und
hüteten sein. Und oben zu
seinen Häupten hefteten sie
die Ursach seines Todes bes-
chrieben, nämlich:
"Dies ist Jesus, der Jüden
König."
Und da wurden zween Mörder
mit ihm gekreuziget, einer zur
Rechten und einer zur Linken.
Die aber vorübergingen,
lästerten ihn und schüttelten
ihre Köpfe und sprachen:

They sat around guarding him
and nailed a sign over his head
announcing the reason for his
execution saying:

"This is Jesus, King of the
Jews."
Two murderers were crucified
alongside Jesus, one on the
right and one on the left.
Those passing by shook their
heads and accused him saying:

Chorus
Der du den Tempel Gottes
zerbrichst und bauest ihn in
dreien Tagen, hilf dir selber!
Bist du Gottes Sohn, so steig
herab vom Kreuz!

You who destroy God's temple
and can build it again in three
days, save yourself!
If you really are the Son of
God, then come down from
that cross!

Evangelist
Desgleichen auch die Hohenpriester spotteten sein samt
den Schriftgelehrten und
Ältesten und sprachen:

The high priests, elders, and
scribes all mocked him along
with the people and said:

Chorus
Andern hat er geholfen und
kann ihm selber nicht helfen.
Ist er der König Israel, so
steige er nun vom Kreuz, so
wollen wir ihm glauben. Er hat
Gott vertrauet, der erlöse ihn
nun, lüstet's ihn; denn er hat
gesagt: "Ich bin Gottes Sohn."

He saved others, but can't
save himself. If he's the King
of Israel, let him come down
from the cross and then we'll
believe! He trusted in God,
let God deliver him now if he
wants him. He said: "I am the
Son of God."

Evangelist

Desgleichen schmaheten ihn auch die Mörder, die mit ihm gekreuziget waren.

The murderers crucified with him also mocked him.

Track 59 (1:25)
No. 59 Recitative (Alto)
(BWV No. 69)

Ach Golgatha, unselges Golgatha!
Der Herr der Herrlichkeit muss schimpflich hier verderben,
Der Segen und das Heil der Welt
Wird als ein Fluch ans Kreuz gestellt.
Der Schöpfer Himmels und der Erden
Soll Erd und Luft entzogen werden.
Die Unschuld muss hier schuldig sterben,
Das gehet meiner Seele nah;
Ach Golgatha, unselges Golgatha!

Ah, Golgotha, tragic Golgotha!
The Lord of Glory must wretchedly die here,
The blessing and salvation of the world
Is nailed to the cross like a curse.
From the Creator of heaven and earth
Earth and air shall be removed.

The innocent must die as if he is guilty,
That cuts deep into my soul;
Ah, Golgotha, tragic Golgotha!

Day 32—Thursday
(3 minutes)

The soloist and chorus take the congregation to the other side of Golgotha, shining hope onto the dim reality of the cross.

The Great Passion

Scripture Reading

No reading

Listening

Gardiner's Recording: Track 60 (3:18)

Libretto

Track 60 (3:18)
No. 60 Aria (Alto and Chorus)
(BWV No. 70)

Alto

Sehet, Jesus hat die Hand,	See, Jesus's hand,
Uns zu fassen, ausgespannt,	Reaching out to us, come!
kommt!	

Chorus

Wohin?	Where to?

Alto

In Jesu Armen Sucht Erlösung,	In his arms we find redemp-
nehmt Erbarmen, suchet!	tion, take his mercy, find it!

Chorus

Wo?	Where?

Alto

In Jesu Armen.	In Jesus's arms.
Lebet, sterbet, ruhet hier,	Living, dying, rest here.
Ihr verlass'nen Küchlein ihr, bleibet.	You lost little chicks, stay.

Chorus

Wo?	Where?

Alto

In Jesu Armen.	In Jesus's arms.

Day 33—Friday
(3 minutes)

One week out from Good Friday, we'll experience the death of Jesus in the oratorio. Here, at the very end, we get his final words. Even in that last moment, humans are misunderstanding him by thinking he is asking for Elijah. They then use their own mistake as an opportunity to mock him further.

Pay attention to Jesus's brief line in No. 61a (BWV No. 71). Bach removes the strings from accompanying Jesus's final words, taking away his deific "halo."[48] We can imagine Jesus hanging on the cross physically exposed and naked, but as we take in the story auditorily, being stripped of the halo becomes a new and stark reminder of all that Jesus laid down for us. His deity, his glory, his power, his relationship to God, he laid them all willingly aside to reconcile God and man.

When the Evangelist translates Jesus's final words, Bach makes a rare move: he shifts to the key of B flat, a key associated with anguish.[49] The Evangelist's recitative has the impact of an aria.

For the fifth and final time we hear the Passion Chorale ("O Sacred Head, Now Wounded"). Bach chooses a particularly soft dynamic to elicit the sorrow of the people standing at the foot of the cross. The quiet brokenness of those who loved him and thought they lost him is unmistakable. According to Dr. Greenberg, this was the first time a chorale had been interpreted with so much depth of emotion. The slow and quiet nature of the chorale is a brief breath of absolute stillness before the chaos of earthquake, ripping curtains, and dead people walking reigns supreme.[50]

The Great Passion

Scripture Reading

Matthew 27:45-50

Listening

Gardiner Recording: Track 61 (2:04), Track 62 (1:09)

Libretto

Track 61 (2:04)
No. 61a-61e Recitative (Evangelist, Jesus, and Chorus)
(BWV No. 71)

Evangelist

Und von der sechsten Stunde an war eine Finsternis über das ganze Land bis zu der neunten Stunde.	From the sixth to the ninth hour there was darkness over all the land.
Und um die neunte Stunde schriee Jesus laut und sprach:	At about the ninth hour Jesus cried out and said:

Jesus

Eli, Eli, lama asabthani?	Eli, Eli, lama asabthani?

Evangelist

Das ist: Mein Gott, mein Gott, warum hast du mich verlassen?	That means: My God, my God, why have you left me?
Etliche aber, die da stunden, da sie das höreten, sprachen sie:	There were some standing there who heard this and said:

154

Chorus

Der rufet dem Elias!

He calls for Elijah!

Evangelist

Und bald lief einer unter ihnen, nahm einen Schwamm und füllete ihn mit Essig und steckete ihn auf ein Rohr und tränkete ihn. Die andern aber sprachen:

Right away one of them ran under him with a vinegar-filled sponge, put it on a staff, and gave it to him to drink. Others said:

Chorus

Halt! lass sehen, ob Elias komme und ihm helfe?

Wait! Let's see if Elijah comes to save him!

Evangelist

Aber Jesus schriee abermal laut und verschied.

Jesus cried aloud again and died.

Track 62 (1:09)
No. 62 Chorale
(BWV No. 72)

Wenn ich einmal soll scheiden,
So scheide nicht von mir,
So tritt du denn herfür!
Wenn mir am allerbängsten
Wird um das Herze sein,
So reiß mich aus den Ängsten

Kraft deiner Angst und Pein!

When I must depart,
Don't leave me,
Stand by me!
When I am most fearful
Of heart,
Then rescue me from the horrors
Of fear and pain by your strength!

Activity

Media

"Watch the Lamb" by Ray Boltz

Take a moment to find "Watch the Lamb," a song by Ray Boltz, on YouTube. You can find the song on the Spotify playlist (see page 202), but if you find it online, the video is wonderful as a dramatization of the crucifixion. The song is written from the perspective of Simon of Cyrene coming into Jerusalem with his small sons to sacrifice lambs for the Passover. Instead, they witness Jesus bearing the cross and being crucified.

Day 34—Saturday

Media Options

Superbook, Season 1, Episode 11 ("He is Risen")
The Chosen, Season 2, Episode 3 ("Matthew 4:24") or Season 2,
Episode 4 ("The Perfect Opportunity")

We are nearing the end of our Lenten season by heading into Holy Week. If you can, watch Season 1, Episode 11 ("He is Risen") from *Superbook* today. This episode covers the events we just walked through in *St. Matthew Passion* and will give your younger kids a very serious and truthful visual of Christ's suffering and death. As always, preview before showing this to young children. The showrunners don't shy away from the physical and emotional grittiness of this moment.

For older children, consider watching various episodes of *The Chosen* that foreshadow Jesus's death and speak to who he is as the Messiah. At the writing of this book, the series is not complete and therefore the story has not yet reached anything surrounding the crucifixion. Until that happens, Season 2, Episode 3 ("Matthew 4:24") gives fodder for discussion about the connection between Jesus's ministry and his physical exhaustion and pain, pain we've seen up close this past week. Season 2, Episode 4 ("The Perfect Opportunity") brings you into direct contact with what the Israelites were expecting of a Messiah and how vastly Jesus veers away from that expectation.

Watch either of these as a family and take time to talk over what your kids are experiencing after hearing the Scripture, listening to Bach's work, and seeing a visual representation of Jesus and his choice to live and die for humanity.

Holy Week

How happy were my part,
If some kind man would thrust his heart
Into these lines; till in heav'n's court of rolls
They were by winged souls
Entred for both, far above their desert!

—George Herbert in "Obedience"

Palm Sunday

Activities

Reading

"The Donkey" by G.K. Chesterton (on facing page)

Listening

The Gray Havens's song "At Last, the King" from the album *Ghost of a King*

Lent has led us to Holy Week. We now continue the preparation for Easter Sunday by recognizing the Holy Days, but not observing them according to strict tradition. Instead, we'll do a bit of a mix between focusing on where Bach has us in the oratorio, reading poetry each day, and observing some of the traditions of Holy Week. By Good Friday we will be at the final point Bach wants to take us in Matthew, stopping short of the resurrection. To hear the celebratory portion of the story, the congregation was expected to come back to church on Easter Sunday for his Easter cantata.

Where we live, we'll grab some palm leaves out of the backyard and recreate the scene of Jesus entering Jerusalem. Many of you will be able to do this at church.

Poem

Start your time together reading the following poem and finish by listening to "At Last, the King" by The Gray Havens.

Many of the poems chosen in this guide are more complex than young children will be able to fully grasp. We still use them in our family and watch year after year as the familiarity of the verse begins to sprout understanding. Today I've selected a poem by G.K. Chesterton that even the smallest child can appreciate with little explanation.

It never ceases to amaze me how God chose to reveal himself to humanity. It is always through the lowliest of people, place, and means. The animal Jesus chose for his triumphal entry into Jerusalem on Palm Sunday is no exception, and today we'll take a moment to remember that ignoble beast. By remembering his lowliness, we are reminded of our own.

The Donkey

G.K. CHESTERTON

When fishes flew and forests walked
    And figs grew upon thorn,
Some moment when the moon was blood
    Then surely I was born.

With monstrous head and sickening cry
    And ears like errant wings,
The devil's walking parody
    On all four-footed things.

The tattered outlaw of the earth,
    Of ancient crooked will;
Starve, scourge, deride me: I am dumb,
    I keep my secret still.

Fools! For I also had my hour;
    One far fierce hour and sweet:
There was a shout about my ears,
    And palms before my feet.

Day 35—Holy Monday
(2 ½ minutes)

On Holy Monday, Jesus cursed the fig tree, cleansed the temple, and defended his authority immediately prior to his arrest and death. It's worth mentioning this to know what is being tradditionally remembered on Holy Monday, but we won't be focusing on any of those events.

Today, Bach uses the music to palpably bring to life the dramatic events that occurred upon Jesus's death, namely the ripping of the veil, the earthquake, and the graves opening up. In the face of this terrifying evidence, people nearby begin to whisper the truth of Jesus's claims. Listen closely to the chorus. Their voices rise and fall at this new recognition of his dominion over earth and death, painting a sound picture of light breaking through the dark.[51] Perhaps that is the light of truth shining into and dispelling the denial of his claim to be the Son of God. Now those witnesses undoubtedly knew he was exactly who he said he was.

Bach's creativity is on full display in the Evangelist's accompanying instrumentation, but you do have to listen quite closely to catch it. During the ripping of the curtain, the cellos use up and down scales violently giving our ears the sensation that we're hearing fabric tear. Then the cellos shift for the earthquake into a slow rise, shaking as they move higher alongside the harpsichord.[52] The music coming into our ears brings alive images of the earth moving beneath us. It may be difficult to hear these nuances on a basic speaker (like ours). Headphones could be useful again today.

The Great Passion

Scripture Reading

Matthew 27:51-58

Listening

Gardiner Recording: Track 63 (2:28)

Libretto

Track 63 (2:28)
No. 63a-63c Recitative (Evangelist and Chorus)
(BWV No. 73)

Evangelist

Und siehe da, der Vorhang im Tempel zerriss in zwei Stück von oben an bis unten aus.
Und die Erde erbebete, und die Felsen zerrissen, und die Gräber täten sich auf, und stunden auf viel Leiber der Heiligen, die da schliefen, und gingen aus den Gräbern nach seiner Auferstehung und kamen in die heilige Stadt und erschienen vielen.
Aber der Hauptmann und die bei ihm waren und bewahreten Jesum, da sie sahen das Erdbeben und was da geschah, erschraken sie sehr und sprachen:

Behold, the temple curtain was torn in two from top to bottom.
There was an earthquake and the cliffs split apart. Graves opened up and out of them rose the bodies of many holy people who were sleeping. They walked into the holy city where many people saw them.

The centurion and those guarding Jesus were very afraid as they witnessed all of this happening. They said:

Chorus

Wahrlich, dieser ist Gottes Sohn gewesen.	Truly, he was the Son of God.

Evangelist

Und es waren viel Weiber da, die von ferne zusahen, die da waren nachgefolget aus Galiläa und hatten ihm gedienet, unter welchen war Maria Magdalena und Maria, die Mutter Jacobi und Joses, und die Mutter der Kinder Zebedäi. Am Abend aber kam ein reicher Mann von Arimathia, der hieß Joseph, welcher auch ein Jünger Jesu war, der ging zu Pilato und bat ihn um den Leichnam Jesu. Da befahl Pilatus, man sollte ihm geben.	There were many women there who had followed him from Galilee and were looking on from a distance. Among them were Mary Magdalene and Mary, the mother of James and Joseph, and the mother of Zebedee's children. In the evening, a rich man named Joseph of Arimathea, who was also a disciple of Jesus, went to Pilate and asked for the body. Pilate gave it to him.

Poem

I'm originally from North Carolina where earthquakes just aren't a thing. Moving to an island that sits right along the Ring of Fire quickly opened my eyes to what life with earthquakes can feel like. Still, the earthquakes we got there were nothing compared to the monsters that happen elsewhere. They would shake violently giving the sensation of being inside a snow globe, roll slowly like swells on the ocean, or an odd mixture of both, but they didn't bring down whole cities nor did they last very long. Most of the destruction was caused by the side effects; landslides and tsunamis that come behind and can wipe out whole villages. Over the more than fifteen years I lived in PNG, I can only remember running out of the house for fear of the earthquake itself a handful of times. The most recent "panic and run" earthquake was just last year. It started as they all do: noticeable, but nothing that concerned me. It lingered and increased its intensity until I found myself yelling at my family to run outside. We careened onto the grass, stumbling down, our bodies totally losing their center of gravity. Once we were securely seated on the rolling waves that used to be our motionless front lawn, we watched the house shift, the ground move, and the truck bounce back and forth while we heard the earth grinding. It terrified us, and we all now have a wary view of each small earthquake that comes to our attention, wondering if that deeply unsettling experience will replicate itself.

No matter how big or small an earthquake is, the very sensation of the earth moving unpredictably under your feet feels like a betrayal. There are many illusions we have in life about our level of control, and the earth staying put underfoot is high on my list. When that illusion is shattered, well, then what? Where do I go when the ground is no longer safe? Where can I run? It's the ground! It's everywhere!

I've often wondered what it was like for the people standing at the cross. Surely they were petrified. To see and feel the very earth under your feet split at Jesus's death and the graves open up releasing long dead people? Yikes!! It's easy to focus on the legitimacy all these wild events place on Jesus and his claims, but sometimes my imagination drifts to how dark and horrifying that must have been for the witnesses.

Today's poem from George MacDonald (on the following page) addresses our fear of the shadows and unknowns in life. It's so easy to doubt God's steadfastness in those out-of-control moments, but God is immutable. He does not change and will continue to be with us, no matter what chaos rains down. The earth can move, and yet our hearts can be still when firmly rooted in him.

Antiphon
George MacDonald

Daylight fades away.
 Is the Lord at hand
In the shadows gray
 Stealing on the land?

Gently from the east
 Come the shadows gray;
But our lowly priest
 Nearer is than they.

It is darkness quite.
 Is the Lord at hand,
In the cloak of night
 Stolen upon the land?

But I see no night,
 For my Lord is here
With him dark is light,
 With him far is near.

List! the cock's awake.
 Is the Lord at hand?
Cometh he to make
 Light in all the land?

Long ago he made
 Morning in my heart;
Long ago he bade
 Shadowy things depart.

Lo, the dawning hill!
 Is the Lord at hand,
Come to scatter ill,
 Ruling in the land?

He hath scattered ill,
 Ruling in my mind;
Growing to his will,
 Freedom comes, I find.

We will watch all day.
 Lest the Lord should come;
All night waking stay
 In the darkness dumb.

I will work all day,
 For the Lord hath come;
Down my head will lay
 All night, glad and dumb.

For we know not when
 Christ may be at hand;
But we know that then
 Joy is in the land.

For I know that where
 Christ hath come again,
Quietness without care
 Dwelleth in his men.

Day 36—Holy Tuesday
(8 minutes)

This day is also known as Fig Tuesday, a moniker it shares with Monday in some traditions. Monday commemorates the moment Jesus cursed the fig tree for not bearing fruit. On Fig Tuesday, we remember his return to Jerusalem when he passed by the same fig tree, at which point the disciples witness its barrenness. We will not be doing anything associated with these traditions, instead choosing to focus on the oratorio and selected poetry.

We left the story yesterday with Jesus's body being given to Joseph of Arimethea but not buried. In that in-between time of coming off the cross but not yet in the tomb, we find these reflective numbers expressing a desire for Jesus to be entombed in our hearts. It's a bit confronting to think of entombing him inside us, and yet the imagery is powerful.

Notice the poetry in the recitative hitting three major points in the Biblical narrative. First, we get allusions to Adam and with that the entrance of sin and the need for a Christly mission. Next, we see Noah represented in the dove which harkens back to the first time God saved humanity through one family line. Finally, we find ourselves at the cross where sin is conquered and mankind saved. The response aria is the last aria of the work. It has the characteristics of a love song composed with a lightness that may remind you of dancing.[53] Not silly dancing, mind you, but dancing, nonetheless. Encourage your family to be uninhibited with the music in whatever way suits them. If it gets them swaying or dancing, all the better, let them go! Taking the work seriously does not mean sitting perfectly still.

The Great Passion

Scripture Reading

No reading

Listening

Gardiner Recording: Track 64 (1:58), Track 65 (5:57)

Libretto

Track 64 (1:58)
No. 64 Recitative (Bass)
(BWV No. 74)

Am Abend, da es kühle war,	In the cool evening,
Ward Adams Fallen offenbar;	Adam's fall was made apparent;
Am Abend drücket ihn der Heiland nieder.	In the evening he was cast down.
Am Abend kam die Taube wieder	In the evening the dove came back
Und trug ein Ölblatt in dem Munde.	Carrying an olive branch in its beak.
O schöne Zeit! O Abendstunde!	O beautiful time! O evening hour!
Der Friedensschluß ist nun mit Gott gemacht,	We now have peace with God,
Denn Jesus hat sein Kreuz vollbracht.	For Jesus endured the cross.
Sein Leichnam kömmt zur Ruh,	His body comes to rest,
Ach! liebe Seele, bitte du,	Ah, dear soul, I ask you,
Geh, lasse dir den toten Jesum schenken,	Go, receive Jesus's sacrifice,
O heilsames, o köstlichs Angedenken!	O pure, o valuable treasure!

Track 65 (5:57)
No. 65 Aria (Bass)
(BWV No. 75)

Mach dich, mein Herze, rein,	Make yourself clean, my heart,
Ich will Jesum selbst begraben.	I will bury Jesus myself.
Denn er soll nunmehr in mir	He shall now be in me
Für und für	Forever and ever
Seine süße Ruhe haben.	Take his delightful rest.
Welt, geh aus, lass Jesum ein!	World, get out, let Jesus in!

Poem

Read the following poem by Louisa May Alcott as another, and perhaps simpler, way for your family to express inwardly what Bach is saying through the soloists today. We are broken people, but God is a healer. He has rectified Adam's fall through the death of Jesus, and now we have pure hearts and peace with God. However, even though we are now covered by Jesus's blood and given new life, our dominion in the kingdom of our own lives is untenable. We need God to lead us to green pastures and right living.

My Kingdom
LOUISA MAY ALCOTT

A little kingdom I possess
Where thoughts and feelings dwell,
And very hard I find the task
Of governing it well;
For passion tempts and troubles me,
A wayward will misleads,
And selfishness its shadow casts
On all my words and deeds.

How can I learn to rule myself,
To be the child I should,
Honest and brave, nor ever tire
Of trying to be good?
How can I keep a sunny soul
To shine along life's way?
How can I tune my little heart
To sweetly sing all day?

Dear Father, help me with the love
That casteth out my fear;
Teach me to lean on thee, and feel
That thou art very near,
That no temptation is unseen
No childish grief too small,
Since thou, with patience infinite,
Doth soothe and comfort all.

I do not ask for any crown
But that which all may win
Nor seek to conquer any world
Except the one within.
Be thou my guide until I find,
Led by a tender hand,
Thy happy kingdom in myself
And dare to take command.

Day 37—Holy Wednesday
(2½ minutes)

Holy Wednesday is also called Spy Wednesday. Traditionally the focus is on Judas Iscariot and his actions as a betrayer and spy amongst the disciples. We are well past this portion of the story, so we won't be focusing there. Instead, we're experiencing the somber event of burying Jesus and watching the women who loved him stand vigil over his tomb.

The Great Passion

Scripture Reading

Matthew 27:59-66

Listening

Gardiner Recording: Track 66 (2:30)

Libretto

Track 66 (2:30)
No. 66a-66c Recitative (Evangelist, Chorus, and Pilate)
(BWV No. 76)

Evangelist

Und Joseph nahm den Leib und wickelte ihn in ein rein Leinwand und legte ihn in sein eigen neu Grab, welches er hatte lassen in einen Fels hauen, und wälzete einen großen Stein vor die Tür des Grabes und ging davon.

Joseph took the body, wrapped it in a clean linen shroud, and laid it in his own new tomb. The tomb was cut inside of a rock and, after a heavy stone was placed in front to seal it, Joseph left.

Es war aber allda Maria Magdalena und die andere Maria, die satzten sich gegen das Grab.

Mary Magdalene came and sat next to the tomb with the other Mary.

Des andern Tages, der da folget nach dem Rüsttage, kamen die Hohenpriester und Pharisäer sämtlich zu Pilato und sprachen:

The next day, the high priests and the Pharisees went to Pilate and said:

Chorus

Herr, wir haben gedacht, dass dieser Verführer sprach, da er noch lebete: Ich will nach dreien Tagen wieder auferstehen. Darum befiehl, dass man das Grab verwahre bis an den dritten Tag, auf dass nicht seine Jünger kommen und stehlen ihn und sagen zu dem Volk: Er ist auferstanden von den Toten, und werde der letzte Betrug ärger denn der erste!

Sir, we remember when this liar said, "I will in three days time stand here resurrected." Therefore, put the tomb under guard until three days have passed so none of his disciples can steal him and make a claim to the people saying, "He's alive and back from the dead." If they convince the people of a lie like that, it will be far worse than what he's already done!

Evangelist

Pilatus sprach zu ihnen:

Pilate said to them:

Pilate

Da habt ihr die Hüter; gehet hin und verwahret's, wie ihr's wisset!

Here, have these guards; go and secure it to the best of your ability!

Evangelist

Sie gingen hin und verwahreten das Grab mit Hütern und versiegelten den Stein.

So they left and secured the tomb with guards. They also sealed the stone door.

Poem

So much of Lent is about being quiet and hearing the story of Jesus's sacrifice anew each year. Allowing it to play on our memories while bringing new understanding is difficult to do, especially if we're busy with life and allowing temporal worries to crowd out quiet truths. The poem today is from Christina Rossetti and asks God for clarity of mind and open ears. Take a moment today before diving into the final days of Holy Week to ask God for ears to hear.

Lord, Grant Us Eyes
CHRISTINA ROSSETTI

Lord, grant us eyes to see and ears to hear,
   And souls to love and minds to understand,
   And steadfast faces toward the Holy Land,
And confidence of hope, and filial fear,
And citizenship where Thy saints appear
   Before Thee heart in heart and hand in hand,
   And Alleluias where their chanting band
As waters and as thunders fill the sphere.
Lord, grant us what Thou wilt, and what Thou wilt
   Deny, and fold us in Thy peaceful fold:
      Not as the world gives, give to us as Thine own:
Inbuild us where Jerusalem is built
   With walls of jasper and with streets of gold,
      And Thou Thyself, Lord Christ, for Corner Stone.

Day 38—Maundy Thursday
(1½ minutes)

Ah! What an ending we start having today and finish tomorrow! Much earlier I mentioned that someone else in the oratorio would receive Jesus's "halo," his string accompaniment. When I first had my family guessing who it would be, they were absolutely flummoxed when we arrived at this point and still had not seen it handed over, but they had some insightful guesses along the way. They underestimated Bach's ability to bring this ancient story into the here-and-now for his audience all the way through to the very end when the story feels done. Jesus laid down the halo with his final words in order to die for mankind. It is now transferred to four soloists in their steadily rising tribute to the work he did on the cross. The solos start with the bass and continue up the scale with tenor followed by the alto and then soprano. It feels as though the voices are soaring up into heaven and bringing us with them!

That halo! Why is it transferred to the soloists today? There are multiple theories amongst Bach scholars, but the one that rings truest to me is that the halo is being passed on to Christians worldwide with the soloists representing them again as the Faithful. (We've seen them before.) The Faithful are covered by his blood and adopted into brotherhood with him, and as such receive the birthright of deity and eternal life; ergo, they receive the symbolic halo.[54] Another compelling theory is that the four soloists represent the four Gospel writers, namely Matthew, Mark, Luke, and John. Those four are commanded and given the authority to "go and make disciples."[55] Either way, it's a powerful reminder of what Jesus did for us and why.

We've had 44 days of intentionally staring down the tragedy of Jesus. We are so very close to celebrating the other side of all this: the dawn of resurrection and our adoption into his sacred family!

The Great Passion

Scripture Reading

No reading

Listening

Gardiner Recording: Track 67 (1:37)

Libretto

Track 67 (1:37)
No. 67 Recitative (Bass, Tenor, Alto, Soprano, and Chorus)
(BWV No. 77)

Bass

Nun ist der Herr zur Ruh gebracht.	Now the Lord is brought to rest.

Chorus

Mein Jesu, gute Nacht!	My Jesus, good night!

Tenor

Die Müh ist aus, die unsre Sünden ihm gemacht.	The work our sins created for him is done.

Chorus

Mein Jesu, gute Nacht!	My Jesus, good night!

Alto

O selige Gebeine,	O blessed bones,
Seht, wie ich euch mit Buß und Reu beweine,	See how I weep for you with such regret and sorrow,
Dass euch mein Fall in solche Not gebracht!	That my mistakes brought you such hardship!

Chorus

Mein Jesu, gute Nacht!

My Jesus, good night!

Soprano

Habt lebenslang
Vor euer Leiden tausend Dank,

Dass ihr mein Seelenheil so
wert geacht'.

Take lifelong
A thousand thanks for your
suffering,

That you value my soul's redemption so highly.

Chorus

Mein Jesu, gute Nacht!

My Jesus, good night!

Activities

In honor of Maundy Thursday, with its focus on the Last Supper and Jesus washing his disciples' feet, our activity will be foot washing. Take time tonight as parents to wash your children's feet while discussing the import of having a servant's heart. In some eras of church history and in varied denominations, *Ubi Caritas* is used during the washing of the feet ceremony. This is a Latin hymn attributed to Paulinus of Aquileia in the late 8th century meaning, "Where true charity is, God is there."

Two versions of this will be available on the Spotify playlist (see page 202) for use while you wash your children's feet. One is a bit more modern and sung by Audrey Assad. The other is more traditional and sung by Ola Gjeilo and Voces. The following lyrics are the original hymn. Both versions on Spotify abridge the song, so don't expect this to match up exactly. In fact, my recommendation is to worry less about strictly listening to the song and instead allow the music in its other-worldliness to permeate your action by playing it in the background.

Ubi Caritas

Ubi cáritas et amor, Deus ibi est.
Congregávit nos in unum Christi amor.
Exultémus, et in ipso iucundémur.
Temeánus et amémus Deum vivum,
Et ex corde diligámus nos sincéro.

Ubi cáritas et amor, Deus ibi est.
Simul ergo cum in unum congregámur:
Ne nos mente dividámur, caveámus.
Cessent iúrgia malígna, cessent lites.
Et in médio nostri sit Christus Deus.

Ubi cáritas et amor, Deus ibi est.
Simul quoque cum beátis videámus
Gloriánter vultum tuum, Christe Deus:
Gáudium, quod est imménsum atque probum.
Sæcula per infiníta sæculórum. Amen.[56]

Day 39—Good Friday
(5 minutes)

Bach finishes the oratorio with both choirs describing that once Jesus defeats death (not until Easter Sunday!), we will rejoice in how he has transformed it. We can return to church on Sunday to celebrate that death is no longer an enemy, but instead the door to eternal life with our Savior. The choices Picander makes in the poetry and Bach makes in musical styles here in the last number are full of cues about how we should emotionally respond to the story.

"My Jesus, good night," was heard again and again yesterday. Today's finale has musical elements of a lullaby as we see Jesus into the abyss.[57] Instead of focusing here at the end on Jesus dying and descending into hell, Picander and Bach are choosing to lean into Jesus being asleep with waking just around the corner. The congregation can leave the church anticipating that awakening on Easter morning. The idea of Jesus sleeping rather than being dead gives a deep hope that though at a very dark end here, it isn't so dark after all. We lament and grieve, but we also hope and look to his return.

The Great Passion

Scripture Reading

No reading

Listening

Gardiner Recording: Track 68 (5:10)

Libretto

Track 68 (5:10)
No. 60 Chorus
(BWV No. 78)

Wir setzen uns mit Tränen nieder	We sit in tears
Und rufen dir im Grabe zu:	And call to you in your tomb:
Ruhe sanfte, sanfte ruh!	Rest peacefully, peacefully rest!
Ruht, ihr ausgesognen Glieder!	Rest, you exhausted bones!
Euer Grab und Leichenstein	Your grave and tombstone
Soll dem ängstlichen Gewissen	Will be for the unsettled conscience
Ein bequemes Ruhekissen	A comfortable pillow
Und der Seelen Ruhstatt sein.	And the soul's resting place.
Höchst vergnügt schlummern da die Augen ein.	In utter joy the eyes close there.

Poem

We're returning to Christina Rossetti for today's poem. Read this at any time, not necessarily along with the song selection. Rossetti ruminates on her tendency to act more like an inflexible rock and less like a malleable sheep. I love what this poem has to say about my own heart at this time of year. I've heard the story more times than I can count, and my heart becomes immune to its overwhelming power. I don't want to be like the stone standing under the cross, feeling nothing, and yet I find myself there being exactly that again and again. Pairing her poem pleading for God to give her ears to hear (the one we read on Holy Wednesday) with this one pleading for God to soften her heart completes my own prayer and the prayer I have for my children: that God would smite this human rock.

Good Friday

CHRISTINA ROSSETTI

Am I a stone and not a sheep
That I can stand, O Christ, beneath thy cross,
To number drop by drop Thy blood's slow loss,
And yet not weep?

Not so those women loved
Who with exceeding grief lamented thee;
Not so fallen Peter weeping bitterly;
Not so the thief was moved;

Not so the sun and moon
Which hid their faces in a starless sky,
A horror of great darkness at broad noon—
I, only I.

Yet give not o'er,
But seek thy sheep, true Shepherd of the flock;
Greater than Moses, turn and look once more
And smite a rock.

Day 40—Holy Saturday

Holy Saturday is part of the *Triduum*, the three days primarily representing Jesus's time in the tomb. It's observed in a myriad of ways, many of which can be easily brought into the home. I'm choosing to highlight the Tenebrae service, an event that occurs in both Protestant and Catholic traditions on varying days. Some churches hold their Tenebrae service early in the week, some hold it on Holy Wednesday, and others observe it during the morning prayers of the Triduum. What I'm recommending for today is an extremely simplified home Tenebrae service that can serve as a sensory-filled and solemn time of preparation for your family's Sunday celebrations.

Tenebrae

To begin with, what is *tenebrae*? Pronounced ten-uh-bray, it's Latin for "shadows" or "darkness." On Holy Saturday we live in the terrifying between. Jesus has died . . . now what?! Now. What! The disciples were scared, confused, grieving, and stunned. None of this had gone how they expected. Saturday can easily be an afterthought, or a day spent busily cleaning for Easter festivities, but it's important to sit in the confusion and fear feeling the somber weight of all that has come before. If you're abstaining from lights at night during Holy Week, the at-home Tenebrae service will be even more meaningful. Typically, during the service, fifteen candles are slowly lit and then extinguished while passages from the Lamentations of Jeremiah are read or sung to the congregation. The last candle, or the Christ candle, is left lit until it's standing alone. At that point it is extinguished or hidden, leaving the church in the shadows and the dark. This represents the death of Christ and signals the *strepitus*, the "loud noise." Long ago congregants would slam their books closed as one. Today there are many different methods of making the noise, but they all symbolize the chaos that occurred as Jesus died, most specifically the earthquake. It's a feast for your ears and eyes.

How can you recreate this simply at home? Turn off all your electric lights and talk to your family about experiencing this day of shadows alongside the frightened disciples. You may want to make your Tenebrae more robust by including passages from Lamentations, but I'll leave that to you. For ours, we listen to Gregorio Allegri's *Miserere Mei*, slowly lighting the candles and then slowly extinguishing the candles. When the song ends, we snuff out the Christ candle and make a loud noise. You might like to include your children in the preparation by getting their ideas for how they would like to make the noise. By including them in the planning, the lighting of the candles, and the extinguishing of the candles, it becomes inviting and personal.

In the Spotify playlist (see page 202), I've included a haunting version of *Miserere Mei*. Allegri composed this song specifically for the Tenebrae service. The lyrics below are from *Year of Wonder* by Clemency Burton-Hill.[58]

Miserere mei, Deus: secundum magnam misericordiam tuam.
Have mercy upon me, O God, after Thy great goodness.

The Tenebrae service ends abruptly with the loud noise leaving you in the same state of grief and confusion the disciples are in before the glorious discovery in the garden. It's meant to feel raw and unfinished because that's exactly what Holy Saturday is about. Let it be that.

Easter Sunday
(20 minutes)

I f you use *Hallelujah: Cultivating Advent Traditions with Handel's Messiah* during Advent, this will be a natural circle back. Today is busy with church services, big meals, and Easter egg hunts, but finding time to sit quietly with this powerful work to herald the victory of Jesus over death is worthwhile. Handel always meant for his oratorio to be an Easter event, so listening to portions of *Messiah* Part 3 honors his original intent. Read the Scripture, listen to the works (tracks are included in "The Sacred Sacrifice" Spotify playlist—see page 202), pray, and get ready to close out Eastertide with souls full of truth and ready to face the Ordinary Time until Advent comes round again.[59]

Soli deo gloria.

He is Risen!

Scripture Reading

Matthew 28

Listening

Selections from Handel's *Messiah*: Nos. 46, 47, 50, 51, 52, and 54

Libretto

No. 46
Aria "I Know That My Redeemer Liveth" (6:17)

I know that my Redeemer liveth,
And that He shall stand at the latter day
Upon the earth.

And though worms destroy this body,
Yet in my flesh shall I see God.
For now is Christ risen from the dead,
The first fruits of them that sleep.

No. 47
Chorus "Since By Man Came Death" (2:12)

Since by man came death,
By man came also the resurrection of the dead.
For as in Adam all die,
Even so in Christ shall all be made alive.

No. 50
Recitative "Then Shall Be Brought to Pass" (:17)

Then shall be brought to pass the saying
That is written:
"Death is swallowed up in victory."

No. 51
Duet "O Death, Where Is Thy Sting?" (1:07)

O death, where is thy sting?
O grave! where is thy victory?
The sting of death is sin,
And the strength of sin is the law.

No. 52
Chorus "But Thanks Be to God" (2:27)

But thanks be to God,
Who giveth us the victory
Through our Lord Jesus Christ.

No. 54
Chorus "Worthy Is the Lamb" (7:21)

Worthy is the Lamb that was slain,
And hath redeemed us to God by His blood,

To receive power, and riches, and wisdom,
And strength, and honor, and glory,
And blessing.
Blessing and honor, glory and power,
Be unto Him that sitteth upon the throne,
And unto the Lamb, for ever and ever. Amen.

Extras

Shrove Tuesday and Easter Recipes

A passion for my husband is cooking food for our family. A passion for me? Avoiding cooking food at all. It works well, especially around holidays, where we divide and conquer the various aspects of life and end up with a well-rounded experience. Almost all the recipes we enjoy on Shrove Tuesday and Easter Day are executed by Brian, so here they are in his words. I've just added two recipes to the mix.

Shrove Tuesday Feast

As my wife was embarking on her journey to help our family better celebrate Easter together through *St. Matthew Passion*, I did what I do creatively. I made food! I started by learning more about Shrove Tuesday and discovered that in England it's called Pancake Day. Perfect! We love pancakes! So now our family's pre-Lent feasting consists of a savory style pancake followed by a dessert pancake. To drink, we have a fruity, minty concoction I quite literally threw together with what I had on hand, but it felt necessary. What is a feast without a drink?

For this feast to work, you should cook both kinds of pancakes and the savory pancake filling well in advance of dinner time. It can even be done the day before. They will all keep just fine in the refrigerator. (Though you should reheat the filling before using.) Both types of pancakes are best served straight out of the pan. I usually cook up one for each person, serve, return to the kitchen, and cook the rest so everyone can have two (or more). Repeat with dessert. This does mean you'll be in the kitchen while everyone gets to enjoy conversation around the food you've cooked, but you can relish in the joy you are bringing to others and recognize that by being in the kitchen alone no one sees how many of the pancakes you eat.

Pancake Day Savory Pancakes

Now these are not your grandma's pancakes—unless your grandma is English. Then they are like them, but they're probably not as good as hers. To an American mindset, these pancakes are more like fat crêpes.

Makes 8-10 Pancakes
½ cup plus 2 tablespoons of plain flour
½ teaspoon of salt
2 eggs
1¼ cups of milk
Little oil for the pan

1. Mix all ingredients except the oil together. Good recipes will tell you to slowly mix the wet and dry ingredients by adding just a little bit of milk at a time, probably to avoid lumps or something. I don't have time for that. Dump it all in a bowl and mix it together. Keep beating until it's smooth; the batter will be runny. Do as you see fit: the Dad dump-it-all way or the proper mix-wet-and-dry-slowly way.

2. Heat your biggest frying pan over medium heat. Splash some oil in there (don't burn yourself) and then ladle batter into the pan. You want to completely cover the bottom of the pan with batter. Carefully pick the pan up and rotate it around to make sure the batter is evenly distributed. Bubbles will start to form. You'll want to flip the pancake once the holes made by the bubbles don't fill back in. Flip it just to set the other side of the pancake and then put it to the side on a plate with a paper towel on it. It will take some time to find the right amount of batter for each one and when to flip. You'll have it mastered by the time you've finished.

3. Now we have a stack of pancakes which are nothing more than a delivery system for other more delicious food. You can get leftovers out of the fridge if you want; you could do a breakfast themed pancake with bacon and eggs; or you could do what I did by making the savory filling on the next page.

Savory Filling

You'll need cooked white rice, steamed broccoli, and grilled chicken. (I find using a lime-heavy marinade for the chicken before grilling is lovely in this application.)

Cooked white rice
Steamed broccoli
Grilled chicken
Little oil for the pan

1. Chop the chicken and broccoli into small pieces and mix it into the rice.
2. Add cheese, if desired.
3. Reheat your pan. Put in a little oil. Add a pancake and then dollop a goodly bit of the filling into the pancake and fold in half. (There is a fancy way to fold it if you'd like, but I prefer this for simplicity.) Move your folded pancake to one side of the pan and add another pancake to the pan, fill it, fold it, and by the time you're done with that you can probably flip the first. Keep doing that until you run out of pancakes.
4. Serve with any sauce to match your filling.

Fruity Minty Drink

At the last minute I decided we needed to have a drink with our feast, so I mixed this together.

2 liters (*or* 2 quarts) pineapple juice
½ cup apple juice
a few drops of mint extract (*Be very careful here because it is powerful.*)
4 or 5 healthy splashes of bitters
a little brown sugar

Mix all ingredients beforehand and get it as cold as you can before serving.

Pancake Day Dessert Pancakes
Makes 8-10 Pancakes

½ cup regular flour
Dash of salt
1 tablespoon of cocoa powder
2 tablespoons of sugar
1 egg
½ cup plus 2 tablespoons of milk
Little oil for the pan

Filling options: Nutella, sliced bananas, strawberries, chocolate,
     jam, peanut butter
Powdered sugar

1. Mix all ingredients together except filling options and
    powdered sugar. Again, just chuck it all in a bowl and mix it
    together until smooth (I typically use a blender to get it extra
    smooth). Properly done? Slowly add wet ingredients to dry.
    This batter will be even thinner than the savory pancakes.
    Same procedure as before: ladle batter into a hot pan with
    a little oil, let it cook, flip it, move it to resting place, repeat
    until you're out of batter.
2. Reheat the pan and this time add a good bit of butter.
    Put a pancake back in and add a spoonful of Nutella and
    sliced bananas. Fold the pancake and then build another.
    Repeat until you've cooked them all. Other fillings could
    be strawberries, chocolate and/or peanut butter instead of
    Nutella, or even some sort of jam.
3. Serve dusted with powdered sugar to make them look all
    fancy!

Easter Sunday Morning

Resurrection Buns

This is one of two recipes that I, Hannah, am contributing. Growing up my parents did Hot Cross Buns occasionally, but it wasn't a tradition. Once my husband and I moved overseas, we didn't focus much on Easter traditions. From our early marriage days, I distinctly remember one of our teammates in PNG making Resurrection Buns each year. They were magical and far superior to Hot Cross Buns in my mind. Have fun with your kids eating these "empty tombs."

Makes 8 Rolls

1 10-ounce can of refrigerated crescent dinner rolls (*This is the easy way. You can use your favorite dinner roll recipe and adjust baking times accordingly.*)

8 large marshmallows

¼ cup butter, melted

¼ cup of cinnamon-sugar, mixed to the proportions you like

1. Preheat the oven to 350°F. Line a baking sheet with parchment paper.
2. Separate the crescent rolls into flat triangles.
3. Dip each marshmallow into the melted butter and then coat with the cinnamon-sugar mixture.
4. Place the marshmallow in the middle of a dough triangle and wrap the crescent roll around it, being sure to seal them well. Pinch the dough shut. (The marshmallow will want to escape during the baking process.)
5. Place the rolls on the baking sheet and bake until golden brown (around 10 minutes). You can keep these in a sealed container for a couple of days, but they're certainly best hot out of the oven!

Easter Dinner

We started this journey with a feast, and we'll end with one. Our feast consists primarily of meat and potatoes with beignets for dessert. My wife will slide in an easy homemade bread recipe. You could add more side dishes as you like. Both of my grandmothers could fill a table with ten or more side dishes, but there are only so many recipes we can put in here.

Daddy's Rustic Mashed Potatoes

Serves: I don't know—something like 5-15 people

A lot of potatoes (2-3 lbs.), cut into cubes
A lot of dairy (approximately 2 cups milk, 1-2 cups shredded cheese, butter, or cream cheese—see below)
Salt, spices, and other things you like in mashed potatoes (Your choice, but I like garlic powder, even a bit of spicy or brown mustard.)

1. Get a bunch of potatoes, like 2 or 3 pounds. Wash them to get most of the dirt off, but don't worry about peeling them. We're going for "rustic style." Cube them up, but don't get too fancy with it.
2. Chuck in enough boiling water to cover the potatoes. Keep boiling them until you can easily stick a fork through it. We're going to hand mash, so you want to think, "Yep, I could mash that pretty easily."
3. Strain the potatoes, being careful of the steam.
4. Put the potatoes into a bowl with a lot of extra space. Now open your fridge. What do you have? Cream cheese? Put the whole tub in. Cheddar cheese? Shred two handfuls and put it on top. Cream? Straight in. Milk? That'll do, too. I try to go for something like 2 cups of liquid dairy and then maybe another cup or two of solid dairy. Can't forget the butter. Maybe like

½ cup of that. Be creative at this point. Do you have Ranch dressing? Squirt it in. Open container of ricotta cheese you used once for lasagna? Now's the time to get rid of it. All cheeses work here; even blue cheese if you like that sort of thing. You should be looking at a bowl of potatoes and dairy.

5. Season the potatoes. It now needs lots of salt. Pepper if you like it, maybe some garlic powder. These should be very much to your taste. One secret ingredient I like to add is a generous squirt of spicy or brown mustard.

6. Now mash it. You can "overwork" potatoes, and you don't want that, so just mash until all the liquid is absorbed and it looks like mashed potatoes. Leave some chunks. It's rustic, remember? If it looks a little dry, you didn't add enough dairy. Add some more, but mix it in with the big wooden spoon your Mama waved around threateningly so you don't overwork the potatoes. Once the consistency is right, you can give it a taste to dial in the salt and flavors you're wanting.

7. If you're trying to up the veggies your kids are eating, you could take some steamed broccoli florets and mix them in. Boom! You've changed this caloric explosion into a healthy side dish. Broccoli does that.

Grilled Whole Chicken

For many families, Easter is a time for some kind of roast or ham—something you put in the oven before church that can be on the table in time for a traditional mid-afternoon feast. It's blazing hot where we live. We avoid using the oven if possible. I prefer using the grill, so I typically cook chicken, but feel free to cook what you like or what you're good at.

Chicken (*We want a whole chicken here.*)
Olive oil
Spices for a dry rub: salt, sugar, garlic powder, coriander, paprika, dry mustard, plus whatever else you would like
Apple juice (about 1 cup)

Fresh herbs (rosemary, basil, thyme)
Plus an empty can (soda can or other empty can)

1. Get everything together and ready before touching the chicken.
2. Make the dry rub. Get out the olive oil and a bunch of spices. Mix together salt, sugar, garlic powder, coriander, paprika, dry mustard and anything else you think would taste good in there. Give it a taste. It should be salty and sweet with a lot of flavor. You'll notice I'm not using measurements because I don't have them. Tasting it is the measuring stick.
3. Prepare the chicken. Now we're ready to handle the chicken. Put it in a pan. Pour some good glugs of olive oil on the chicken. Using only one hand, rub the oil in on all sides of the chicken. Now with your non-chicken hand, pick up the bowl of rub and pour it on. Use your chicken hand to massage the rub everywhere. You want a good covering. Now wash your hands thoroughly! Salmonella is not okay on Easter.
4. Find an empty can of some kind. This can be a soda can or something of that size. Fill it halfway with apple juice or a similarly colored liquid. Throw some fresh rosemary, basil, or thyme herbs in there if you have them.
5. Now heat the grill. Whether you're using coal or gas, you're going to want to set it up so that you have a hot fire on one side. The chicken is going to be on the other side. So either build your fire to one side or use the burners on only one side of the grill. Once the grill is preheated, you're going to take your apple juice herb can and put it upright on a pan. Then take your chicken and slide it down onto the can so it's standing. Use the chicken legs as a tripod. Now put it on the cool side of the grill, straight on the rack. Let it sit for an hour and then check. Chicken has to get to 165° F to be safe to eat. I usually pull it off when it hits 160° or so because the temperature will continue to go up. One of those probe thermometers that you can leave in the chicken while it cooks

and check without opening the lid of the grill is worth its weight in gold here.

6. When it's ready, pull it out onto a pan and let it rest 5-10 minutes. Be careful with the can as the metal will be very hot to touch, and it will contain hot liquid. Carve it up!

Juliann's Bread

I (Hannah) have vivid memories of my early days in PNG, before I was married, when I would lie shoulder to shoulder with Juliann, my team-mate and dear friend, staring up at our thatched roof listening to geckos scrabbling around while the daily rhythms of village life swirled below us. We watched the sunlight dance through the cracks taking turns reading James Herriot chapters aloud to each other and felt oh-so-far-away from everything that felt familiar and safe. We were both young and single back then, and we somehow survived village living together. In fact, we walked away closer than before. That is a sacred time in my life that will always and only belong to the two of us. The things we experienced, the fights we had over how you properly wash pans in a river, the hair braiding, the tears, all of it; we could tell you about it, but none of it would shape your soul the way it did ours. I can share our culinary delight, though. Food became a certain solace to us when everything else was chaotic. Juliann is a brilliant cook, and she blessed my tummy with this recipe way back then in a remote PNG village. We baked it in a drum oven over a fire, so this is a hardy piece of work. I brought it with me into married and mom life as a quick and simple homemade bread option. Enjoy!

Makes two loaves

1 tablespoon of yeast
2 cups of warm water (110° F)
½ cup of sugar
⅓ cup of oil
½ tablespoon of salt
6 cups flour

1. Preheat the oven to 375°F.
2. Dissolve the yeast into the warm water.
3. Add the sugar, oil, and salt.
4. Slowly add flour and knead for 5-10 minutes.
5. Let the dough rise in a warm spot for one hour, punch down and form into two loaves. Once they're settled in your loaf pans, let them rise again. You'll know they're ready when you gently press with two fingers, and the dough rebounds slowly (rather than quickly).
6. Bake for 30-45 minutes or until golden brown.

Beignets

How about a Mardi Gras dessert to close out the Easter season? Pronounced ben-yay, *these fried dough pillows are straight from New Orleans and perfect at putting on any weight you may have lost fasting.*

Serves 8 (16 beignets)

3 cups of white flour
¾ teaspoon of salt
3 tablespoons of sugar, divided
1 cup of warm milk, about 110°F
2 teaspoons of dry yeast
1 egg
3 tablespoons of butter, melted
Enough oil to fry

1. Bloom the yeast in the milk with one tablespoon of sugar in a small bowl. Mix that all together and wait until it gets foamy, five minutes or so.
2. Mix the flour, salt, and remaining sugar in a bowl. Set aside.
3. Once the yeast is ready, mix the egg into it.
4. Add it to the dry ingredients from step 2. Use a spoon, or your hand, or your stand mixer to bring it together into a

dough. Add the melted butter and mix some more until it is incorporated.

5. Use the hook attachment for your mixer or elbow grease to knead the dough. Knead for 6 minutes or so. The dough should be tacky but not wet.

6. Get another bowl and grease it with a little spray of oil. Shape your dough into a ball and put it in the bowl. Cover with a tea towel and let rise until it's doubled in size. This could take 1 or 2 hours depending on how hot your kitchen is.

7. After dinner, get your fryer out, or a large pot, and fill it with oil. Start heating the oil to 325°F. You'll want a baking sheet right next to you on the counter with a cooling rack set up in it. Have your tongs ready as well.

8. Turn the dough out onto a floured surface and roll it into a weird cloud shape to about a quarter-inch thick. Cut it into little squares, triangles, and rounded rectangles.

9. Fry it in batches, turning over when golden brown (90 seconds or so per side). Put onto the cooling rack on the baking sheet when done.

10. While they're still searing hot, squeeze a very healthy amount of honey onto them. You may have noticed that this isn't a very sweet dough. As they cool, transfer them to your serving plate and hit them with a good dusting of powdered sugar.

Enrichment Resources

Here are some excellent resources if you'd like to go further.

Applegate, Celia. *Bach in Berlin: Nation and Culture in Mendelssohn's Revival of the St. Matthew Passion*. Cornell University Press, 2014.
If you're a history buff and get really interested in the role of St. Matthew Passion in the overall resurgence of Bach as well as nationalism in Germany, then give this book a go. It's well written, and though dense, it was fascinating. I love history.

Guite, Malcolm. *The Word in the Wilderness: A Poem a Day for Lent and Easter*. Hymns Ancient & Modern Ltd, 2014.
Malcolm Guite's poetry is food for the soul, but in this collection, he includes poems from many other poets as well.

Rollins, Cindy. *Hallelujah: Cultivating Advent Traditions with Handel's Messiah*. Blue Sky Daisies, 2023.
A listening guide for Advent using the Messiah. Rollins includes ideas for family Advent traditions, recipes, hymns, and poems to memorize as you walk through the oratorio and prepare for Christmastide.

Ryken, Leland. *The Soul in Paraphrase*. Crossway, 2018.
Another poetry anthology that includes explanations and historical context for the chosen poems.

Venezia, Mike. "Getting to Know the World's Greatest Composers: Leonard Bernstein" Children's Press, 2017.
This is another in that favored picture book biography series. If you listen to Bernstein's 1963 performance, try to include this as a read-aloud at some point.

Sources

Applegate, Celia. *Bach in Berlin: Nation and Culture in Mendelssohn's Revival of the St. Matthew Passion*. London: Cornell University Press, 2014.

Bostridge, Ian, Ton Koopman, Joshua Rifkin, and Christophe Wolff, "A Visitor's Guide to the St. Matthew Passion," interview by Lynn Neary, Milestones of the Millennium, NPR, March 18, 2008, audio, 50:20, https://www.npr.org/2008/03/18/88203558/a-visitors-guide-to-the-st-matthew-passion.

Burton-Hill, Clemency. *Year of Wonder: Classical Music to Enjoy Day by Day*. New York: HarperCollins, 2018.

Carpenter, Humphrey. *The Inklings: C.S. Lewis, J.R.R. Tolkien, Charles Williams and their Friends*. London: Harper Collins, 2006.

Conlan, James. "Music Director James Conlon's St. Matthew Passion Pre-show Talk." LA Opera. March 11, 2022. Educational video, 34:28. https://www.youtube.com/watch?v=_XvKEO-45Jro&t=2s.

Daniels, Charles. "Daniels on Bach St Matthew Passion BWV 244." Netherlands Bach Society. April 4, 2019. Educational video. 5:16. https://www.youtube.com/watch?v=CC93_G3FgTY&t=1s.

Gardiner, John Elliot. *Music in the Castle of Heaven: A Portrait of Johann Sebastian Bach*. UK: Penguin Random House, 2013.

Greenberg, Dr. Robert. "Bach and the High Baroque." In The Great Courses: Fine Arts & Music, Lectures 25-28. University of California Berkeley: Audible, 2013.

Gilchrist, James. "A Guide to Bach's St. Matthew Passion." KingsCollegeChoir. May 7, 2020. Educational video. 32:05. https://www.youtube.com/watch?v=591fCQvRjmo&t=1421s.

Lederer, Victor. *A Closer Look: Bach's St. Matthew Passion*. New York: The Continuum International Publishing Group Inc, 2008.

Ryken, Leland. *The Soul in Paraphrase: A Treasury of Classic Devotional Poems.* Illinois: Crossway, 2018.

Sato, Shunske. "Sato on Bach St Matthew Passion BWV 244." Netherlands Bach Society. April 3, 2019. Educational video. 7:34. https://www.youtube.com/watch?v=ak0Pxyt9Qfw&t=45s.

Shakespeare, William. *Shakespeare Volume II: The Histories.* London: Heron Books, 1970.

Tolsma Productions. "Bach, Mendelssohn and the Saint Matthew Passion." Mendelssohn Club of Philadelphia and the Chamber Orchestra of Philadelphia. February 6, 2015. Educational video. 20:21. https://www.youtube.com/watch?v=UfNjEykm-WAA&t=1s.

Van Veldhoven, Jos. "Van Veldhoven on Bach St Matthew Passion BWV 244." Netherlands Bach Society. April 6, 2019. Educational video. 4:59. https://www.youtube.com/watch?v=53VrYf_8B0I.

Wolff, Christophe. *Johann Sebastian Bach: The Learned Musician.* New York: W.W. Norton & Company, 2013.

Listening Online

The recommended music audio throughout this book is gathered in a Spotify playlist for your convenience. Add the playlist to your Spotify library using the QR code link below, or search for "The Sacred Sacrifice" playlist by Hannah Paris in the Spotify search function. Alternatively, the albums and songs referenced in this book can be found through other audio platforms when you search for the album or song title referenced.

"The Sacred Sacrifice" Spotify Playlist

Endnotes

1. Celia Applegate, *Bach in Berlin: Nation and Culture in Mendelssohn's Revival of the St. Matthew Passion* (London: Cornell University Press, 2014), chap. 1, Kindle.

2. Carl Ludwig Hilgenfeldt, *Johann Sebastian Bachs Leben, Wirken und Werke* (1850), quoted in Gardiner, *Music in the Castle of Heaven: A Portrait of Johann Sebastian Bach*, 199.

3. John Elliot Gardiner, *Music in the Castle of Heaven: A Portrait of Johann Sebastian Bach* (UK: Penguin Random House, 2013), 91.

4. Gardiner, *Music in the Castle of Heaven*, 55.

5. Christophe Wolff, *Johann Sebastian Bach: The Learned Musician* (New York: W.W. Norton & Company, 2013), 14.

6. Gardiner, *Music in the Castle of Heaven*, 170-171.

7. Gardiner, *Music in the Castle of Heaven*, 172.

8. Gardiner, *Music in the Castle of Heaven*, 125-126.

9. Gardiner, *Music in the Castle of Heaven*, 158.

10. Gardiner, *Music in the Castle of Heaven*, 178.

11. Wolff, *The Learned Musician*, 288.

12. Wolff, *The Learned Musician*, 298.

13. Robert Greenberg, "Bach and the High Baroque," in *The Great Courses: Fine Arts & Music* (University of California Berkeley: Audible, 2013), Lecture 25.

14. Gardiner, *Music in the Castle of Heaven*, 413.

15. Greenberg, "Bach and the High Baroque," Lecture 25.

16. Victor Lederer, *A Closer Look: Bach's St. Matthew Passion* (New York: The Continuum International Publishing Group Inc, 2008), 125.

17. Lederer, *A Closer Look*, 128.

18. Douglas Kaine McKelvey, *Every Moment Holy*, 3 vols. (Every Moment Holy, 2017-2023).

19. Greenberg, "Bach and the High Baroque," Lecture 25.

20. William Shakespeare, *The Life of King Henry V*, (London: Heron Books, 1970), Prologue.

21. Greenberg, "Bach and the High Baroque," Lecture 25.

22. Greenberg, "Bach and the High Baroque," Lecture 26.

23. Greenberg, "Bach and the High Baroque," Lecture 26.

24. Greenberg, "Bach and the High Baroque," Lecture 26.

25. Greenberg, "Bach and the High Baroque," Lecture 26.

26. Greenberg, "Bach and the High Baroque," Lecture 26.

27. Greenberg, "Bach and the High Baroque," Lecture 26.

28. Humphrey Carpenter, *The Inklings: C.S. Lewis, J.R.R. Tolkien, Charles Williams and their Friends* (London: Harper Collins, 2006), 223.

29. Greenberg, "Bach and the High Baroque," Lecture 26.

30. Greenberg, "Bach and the High Baroque," Lecture 26.

31. Leland Ryken, *The Soul in Paraphrase: A Treasury of Classic Devotional Poems* (Illinois: Crossway, 2018), 197.

32. Dr. Robert Greenberg, *The Great Courses: Fine Arts & Music*, "Bach and the High Baroque" (University of California Berkeley: Audible, 2013), Lecture 27.

33. Greenberg, "Bach and the High Baroque," Lecture 27.

34. Greenberg, "Bach and the High Baroque," Lecture 27..

35. Ryken, *The Soul in Paraphrase*, 53.

36. Greenberg, "Bach and the High Baroque," Lecture 27.

37. Greenberg, "Bach and the High Baroque," Lecture 27.

38. Greenberg, "Bach and the High Baroque," Lecture 27.

39. Lederer, *A Closer Look*, 80.

40. Greenberg, "Bach and the High Baroque," Lecture 27.

41. Lederer, *A Closer Look*, 80.

42. Greenberg, "Bach and the High Baroque," Lecture 28.

43. Greenberg, "Bach and the High Baroque," Lecture 28.

44. Greenberg, "Bach and the High Baroque," Lecture 28.

45. Greenberg, "Bach and the High Baroque," Lecture 28.

46. Gilchrist, James. *A Guide to Bach's St Matthew Passion* (YouTube video from KingsCollegeChoir uploaded on 7 May 2020 and accessed on 2 April 2023).

47. Dr. Robert Greenberg, *The Great Courses: Fine Arts & Music*, "Bach and the High Baroque" (University of California Berkeley: Audible, 2013), Lecture 28.

48. Lederer, *A Closer Look*, 95.

49. Greenberg, "Bach and the High Baroque," Lecture 28.

50. Greenberg, "Bach and the High Baroque," Lecture 28.

51. Greenberg, "Bach and the High Baroque," Lecture 28.

52. Lederer, *A Closer Look*, 97.

53. Greenberg, "Bach and the High Baroque," Lecture 28.

54. Greenberg, "Bach and the High Baroque," Lecture 28.

55. Gardiner, *Music in the Castle of Heaven*, 427.

56. A rough, literal translation of *Ubi Caritas* follows:

> Where charity and love are, God is.
> We gather as one in the love of Christ.
> Let us exalt him, and in him be pleased.
> Let us fear and let us love the Living God,
> And out of a sincere heart, let us love one another.
>
> Where charity and love are, God is.
> At the same time, therefore, we are gathered into one.
> Let us be careful not to be divided in mind,
> Let evil quarrels end; let controversy end,
> And in our midst let Christ be God.
>
> Where charity and love are, God is.
> At the same time, let us see with the blessed
> Your face in glory, Christ our God:
> The joy that is immense and good.
> Ages through infinite ages. Amen.

57. Greenberg, "Bach and the High Baroque," Lecture 28.

58. Clemency Burton-Hill, *Year of Wonder: Classical Music to Enjoy Day by Day* (New York: HarperCollins, 2018) chap. title "7 February: Miserere by Grigorio Allegri (c. 1582-1652)," Kindle.

59. In the Lutheran tradition, Eastertide is the 50 days of feasting and celebration following Lent. Pentecost is recognized on the seventh Sunday after Easter Sunday, and is immediately followed by Ordinary Time. During Ordinary Time, we're meant to take all we've learned throughout the liturgical year thus far and live out those principles in our daily lives. We're also meant to take time to intentionally study the life of Jesus. The term "ordinary" here doesn't not mean plain, but instead refers to the numbering of each Sunday throughout this time.

Acknowledgments

When I first set out to write a Lent guide for our family, I had no idea where it would end. There are several people I'd like to acknowledge for their part in transforming my rudimentary plan into a book that will hopefully enliven Bach and Easter for many families. The first is Mirjam Nuessle, my dear friend from our days raising littles in Madang, Papua New Guinea (PNG). She just happens to be German, and she just happened to be willing to help me with the English translation of the libretto. It is far more accurate linguistically and theologically thanks to her valuable input. I also want to thank Kaitlin Silvey for her time reading and editing the manuscript, and cheering me on. Again, the whole thing is vastly improved for your mark on it. Finally, I would be remiss to not acknowledge my husband and three girls. They "strengthened my back," a saying in PNG meaning "to support." Only it's more than that. Quite literally it means to hold another up by pushing their back—being a post holding them firm when they cannot stand alone. The plan would not exist without my girls, and the book would not exist without my husband.

About the Author

After many years in the jungles of Papua New Guinea, Hannah Paris and her family now live with the koalas and wallabies in Far North Queensland, Australia. She and her husband started their lives together as sociolinguistic researchers in a Bible translation organization. After publishing several academic papers and falling into a village pit toilet, Hannah put her research and trekking days behind her in favor of a new adventure: becoming a parent and home educating three lovely girls. She and her husband continue to work in Bible translation from their home in Australia while homeschooling those girls, swimming on Christmas Day, avoiding all the poisonous creatures, and cuddling their puppies, Tumtum and Nutmeg. You can read more from Hannah about homeschooling, missions, and life overseas on their ministry website www.theparisfamily.com.

Discover More from Blue Sky Daisies

Your Lenten season has been enriched with Bach's *St. Matthew Passion*. Experience the Advent season with the companion book *Hallelujah: Cultivating Advent Traditions with Handel's Messiah* by Cindy Rollins. Find out more about *Hallelujah* at BlueSkyDaisies.net.

Umbrellas by Twila Farmer
The traditional art of handmade umbrellas is found in various places in East Asia. *Umbrellas* tells the story of a young girl as she watches her mother, who makes homemade umbrellas in her homeland of Northern Thailand. These beautifully handcrafted umbrellas are a protection from the sun and rain, but they are more than mere umbrellas, they are works of art. This delightful book, written and illustrated by Twila Farmer, will take you along as a girl and her mother create colorful, hand-painted umbrellas in a process filled with skill, creativity, and joy.

Beyond Mere Motherhood by Cindy Rollins
Being a mom can sometimes feel like an overwhelming job with endless tasks and lofty, unattainable goals. It's not easy mothering children.

In the throes of motherhood, moms often find themselves forgetting something foundational to their own identity: moms are people too. This is a book for mothers, but not about mothering. It's a book about education, but not about teaching children. This is a book about self-education. It is a book about how a mother can capture her moments and days in such a way that they add up to a life worth living. Her life. Moms are people too.

More from Cindy Rollins

Morning Time: A Liturgy of Love
The Morning Time Student Anthology
The Literary Life Commonplace Books
The Literary Life KIDS Commonplace Books

Charlotte Mason

Charlotte Mason: The Teacher Who Revealed Worlds of Wonder by Lanaya Gore and illlustrated by Twila Farmer
The Charlotte Mason Book of Quotes: Copywork to Inspire by Lanaya Gore

CopyWorkBook

The CopyWorkBook: Writings of Charlotte Mason by Lanaya Gore
The CopyWorkBook: George Washington's Rules of Civility & Decent Behavior in Company and Conversation by Amy M. Edwards and Christina J. Mugglin
The CopyWorkBook: Comedies of William Shakespeare by Amy M. Edwards and Christina J. Mugglin

Geography Books

Elementary Geography by Charlotte Mason
Home Geography for Primary Grades with Written and Oral Exercises by C. C. Long

Language Arts and Grammar Books

The Mother Tongue: Adapted for Modern Students by George Lyman Kittredge.
In this series: *Workbook 1 and 2; Answer Key 1 and 2*
Exercises in Dictation by F. Peel
Grammar Land: Grammar in Fun for the Children of Schoolroom Shire (Annotated) by M. L. Nesbitt. Annotated by Amy M. Edwards and Christina J. Mugglin

Made in United States
North Haven, CT
12 February 2024

48656541R00117